DAYS WITH

LAL BAHADUR SHASTRI

GLIMPSES FROM THE LAST
SEVEN YEARS

LAL BAHADUR SHASTRI

DAYS WITH
LAL BAHADUR SHASTRI
GLIMPSES FROM THE LAST SEVEN YEARS

RAJESHWAR PRASAD

ALLIED PUBLISHERS PRIVATE LIMITED
NOIDA • MUMBAI • KOLKATA • CHENNAI • BANGALORE

ALLIED PUBLISHERS PRIVATE LIMITED

D-5, Sector-2, **Noida**–201 301
Ph.:0120-4320295/2542557/4352866
• E-mail: delhi.books@alliedpublishers.com

17 Chittaranjan Avenue, **Kolkata**–700072
Ph.: 033-22129618 • E-mail: cal.books@alliedpublishers.com

15 J.N. Heredia Marg, Ballard Estate, **Mumbai**–400001
Ph.: 022-42126969 • E-mail: mumbai.books@alliedpublishers.com

No. 25/10 Commander-in-Chief Road, Ethiraj Lane (Next to Post Office) Egmore, **Chennai**–600008
Ph.: 044-28223938 • E-mail: chennai.books@alliedpublishers.com

P.B No. 9932, No. 15, 3rd Floor (Next to Vijaya Bank), 5th Cross, Gandhinagar, Karnataka, **Bangalore**–560009
Ph.: 080-41530285 / 22386239
• E-mail: bngl.journals@alliedpublishers.com / apsabng@airtelmail.in

Website: www.alliedpublishers.com

First published, 1991
First reprint, 2025

ISBN 10: 81-7023-331-3

ISBN 13: 978-81-7023-331-2

Published by Sunil Sachdev and printed by Ravi Sachdev
at Allied Publishers Pvt. Ltd. D-5, Sector-2, Noida 201 301

To

ARUNA

who longed for me to write books

she was fated never to read

CONTENTS

ACKNOWLEDGEMENTS

MY GRATEFUL acknowledgements to all those who made the writing and publication of these brief recollections possible. Firstly, my sons Ajay Prasad, IAS and Alok Prasad, IFS who went through the first drafts and helped in the typing out of the manuscripts. Ajay, in particular, got the final draft prepared, and then took on himself the tedious and time-consuming but none the less all-important task of going through the proofs. Many of his suggestions proved to be of great value, and in this publication he has been a significant contributor.

The excellent preparation of the typescript and binding of the final draft was done with devotion and dedication by Shri B.D. Gupta and Shri Atma Ram.

To my erstwhile colleague on Shastriji's Personal Staff Shri Jagannath Sahai, I am beholden for the graphic account of the tragic sequence of events at Tashkent during the fatal visit in January 1966. To him as well as to another colleague on the Personal Staff, Shri H.R. Nanda, my grateful thanks for having readily made available some of the photographs from their carefully-treasured collections.

I am greatly obliged to my close friend and former colleague, Shri Kuldip Nayar, and to Shri D.S. Mehta, Adviser, Public Relations, ASSOCHAM without whose help this publication would not have been possible. Kuldip was ever ready to help even when he was in the U.K. Shri Mehta was, as always, forthcoming with his sound advice and wise guidance, and this book owes much to his generous efforts.

The publishers of this book, Allied Publishers, have been a beacon ray of hope and encouragement at a time when one had begun to wonder whether all this effort of remembering and writing was not a case of 'Love's Labour Lost'. I do not think I can be too grateful for their generosity in taking up this publication, and earlier that of a collection of Hindi poems *Lal Chunariya* published posthumously of my late wife Smt. Aruna Prasad.

In writing of Lal Bahadurji, I could not help remembering at every stage the members of his family from whom I have always received so much kindness and affection, and especially Mataji (Smt. Lalita Shastri) who has been a real source of inspiration.

Finally, my deep gratitude to those innumerable persons who having been eager and enthusiastic listeners at my talks on Shastriji, more or less pushed and prodded me into putting these reminiscences down in writing. They have been my motivation.

CHAPTER 1

"THE LITTLE EARTHEN LAMP"

IT IS a strange fact that so little is known about the nature and character of Shri Lal Bahadur Shastri, the second Prime Minister of India. And this despite the fact that he answered in so magnificent a manner the question which had tormented the whole country for well nigh a decade—namely, "After Nehru, who?" As might be recalled, anyone who wrote about India in the late fifties or early sixties—whether they were foreigners like Michael Brecher or Welles Hangen or Indian writers—they all posed this question as crucial for the future of Indian democracy, and attempted their own answers. In a lighter vein an answer was suggested by one of my distinguished predecessors, the first Director of the National Academy of Administration, Mussoorie, the late Shri Aditya Nath Jha, later Lt.-Governor of Delhi. When asked why he had given up the prestigious post of Director of the National Academy in Mussoorie to take up the post of Additional Secretary in the Planning Commission in Delhi, he replied with his characteristic humour: "You see, after some time all the District Magistrates, all the Superintendents of Police, all the Heads of Departments, all the Secretaries to Government, all the Heads of Embassies abroad would have been those who had been trained by me, and the politicians began to fear that the country would have found the answer to 'After Nehru, who?'"

Partly this lack of knowledge about Lal Bahadurji is due to his own shy and retiring nature, which shunned personal publicity. That is why quite a number even today regard him as a rather dull and prosaic sort of person, who rose to the highest post in Government only because of his non-controversial nature, and because of a fortuitous set of circumstances. This impression is heightened by the contrast with the many-splendoured personality of Jawaharlal Nehru, who bestrode the Indian firmament like a Colossus. Shastriji had no such pretensions, nor did he ever attempt or aspire to the dominant position of his giant predecessor. But in his own quiet, reserved, steady manner he sought to discharge the heavy responsibility cast on him, to the best of his ability and with complete integrity. One likes to think of the succession of the charismatic Pt. Jawaharlal Nehru by the quiet and self-effacing Lal Bahadur Shastri in terms of the beautiful and moving poem of Gurudev Rabindranath Tagore: The sun is setting and everyone is worried as to what will happen when darkness will fall. Then the little earthern lamp speaks up: "Light me, and as long as I last, I will do the best I can". This poem is particularly moving in this context, because this is precisely what Shastriji did in the short span of life vouchsafed to him as Prime Minister of India.

In writing about Lal Bahadurji, I am in no way attempting a biography, or even trying to chronicle a list of his achievements. I am confining myself to giving some personal glimpses of his character and personality viewed at close quarters over a period of 7 years. These were the last and most momentous years of his life, when he rose higher and higher up to the very summit, and then suddenly and dramatically vanished from the scene. Even from this brief and somewhat fragmentary account, it will be seen how wrong are those who regard him as a prosaic and colourless sort of person. One may see emerging a very warm human figure, full of wit and humour and the joy of living. And one may get glimpses of the qualities that took him from humble beginnings to the most important and prestigious post this country has to offer.

I had made it a point, as Director of the Lal Bahadur Shastri National Academy of Administration, Mussoorie, for nearly 4 years, to speak to successive batches of trainees about the qualities of the man whose name the institution was privileged to bear. I had kept urging that if only they would remember and put into practice some of his qualities, they would themselves go far in their careers, and would also help to make the country a better place to live in. And most of all, I used to emphasize that if he who rose from humble beginnings to the top-most position, could preserve his humility and humanity to the very end, there was no reason why any of us should lose ours on becoming Class-I officers of the Central Government.

In my own humble way, I think I can claim to be in a unique position to speak and write about him, because I worked with him for seven long years. I joined him as Private Secretary to the Minister of Commerce & Industry on the 11th January 1959, and by a strange and sad coincidence, he departed from this life on the 11th January, 1966. It was 7 years of a rich and rewarding experience, but also 7 years of a tortured existence. The role of a Special Assistant or Private Secretary to a Minister is a combination of the sublime and the ridiculous. He is often the Minister's closest confidant in all official matters and is in touch with issues that even the Secretary to Government in the Ministry knows little about. At the same time, as the nominal head of the Personal Office, he has to keep his eyes and ears close to the ground and keep himself posted with what is happening not only amongst the personal staff—all of them with close and direct links to the Minister—but also in the household. Also, most of the time he has to keep walking on an extremely tight rope, balancing his absolute loyalty to the Minister who trusts him, without displeasing the very highly placed officers of his Service who man the senior posts in the Ministry, and would sometimes like him to get some of their pet proposals approved by the Minister. Occasionally, the situation would become quite difficult, but the guiding principle was never to do anything which would let down the Minister. All in all, the experience was such that one can get in no other post. Apart from being associated with and seeing Shastriji in a period of his continual rise to ever greater heights of power and responsibility, I had also the privilege of seeing from close quarters the top direction of two wars in which India was engaged—The War with China in 1962 and the War with Pakistan in 1965. But Shastriji's methods of working, and his habit of sitting till very late at night in office, night after weary night, made this rich experience also a tormented existence, which I would not care to repeat even for the reward of the seven heavens.

CHAPTER 2

LAL BAHADUR: THE MAN

ON HIS early life I need not dwell much, because it has already been touched upon by those who have written about him, especially the swimming of the Ganga incident. Having lost his father as an infant, his mother's influence was strong upon him and to the very end he faithfully followed the advice she had given him when he had announced his intention of joining the freedom struggle: "Think well and decide, but once having decided, never turn back."

From an early age he was involved in the National Movement, and to the end of his life he remained a member of the Servants of the People Society founded by Lala Lajpat Rai. This membership had a deep influence on him and instilled the spirit of service which was so characteristic of him. Like others who took part in the freedom struggle, he had his share of suffering and sacrifice. But, as will be mentioned in his letter to me, the help and co-operation of his wife went a long way to make the burden bearable. Of his prison days Shastriji used to say that some of his fellow prisoners had begun to almost dread the days when their family members were permitted to visit them. Very often there used to be reproaches to the effect that you are sitting comfortably in jail getting two square meals a day, while the family and children are almost starving, and having a bitter struggle for even bare necessities. But Shastriji said that on such occasions whenever he asked his wife whether she was facing any difficulty she used to smile broadly and say "None at all. There is now one person less to eat".

But of suffering there was no dearth, which can be illustrated by just one instance, which Smt. Shastri once related. Shastriji was in jail when his little daughter fell seriously ill. The doctors said it was typhoid, and the child was unlikely to survive. Even so, Shastriji was unwilling to apply for parole; but at the intervention of some persons the jail authorities permitted him to visit his dying daughter. Perhaps happiness at her father's presence made the child linger on and on, and delayed the inevitable end. Came the last night, when the next morning Shastriji had to return to prison. Smt. Lalita Shastri was faced with the terrible prospect of having to arrange herself for the funeral rites of her child. As she said' "All that night I kept praying to my God. Other mothers pray for the long life of their children; I was praying for the death of mine. God heard my prayers, and the child passed away in the early hours of the morning, and Shastriji was able to perform the last rites before going back to prison".

However, to come to Shastriji himself, the lasting impression one has of him is his essential goodness. He was in every sense of the word one of God's good men, full of compassion and the milk of human kindness. Never did he wish ill to others, and he always recoiled from giving pain. For one who was the Home Minister and Prime Minister of India he could not always avoid doing so, but never did he consciously desire it. And whenever he did come to know of any hurt caused to somebody by any action of his, he agonized over it, sometimes to the extent of making himself miserable. Always, and to all matters, he sought to bring the healing touch.

His goodness found its base in his gentleness and humility, his simplicity and shining integrity. The last few years of his life were those of constant rise, but the pleasures and privileges of office sat lightly on him. One is reminded of the Roman farmer, Cincinnatus who, when the enemies of Rome were at its gates, answered the call of duty and led the armies of Rome to victory, and thereafter returned to the quiet and anonymity of his fields. Like Cincinnatus of old, Shastriji would have been glad to return to his role of a quiet, constructive worker. In his own quiet, humorous way he put it very nicely when after laying the foundation of Mangalore Port as Minister without Portfolio in early 1964, he visited Bangalore. He was presented with a Civic Address by the Bangalore Corporation, on which occasion the Congress President, Shri Kamaraj Nadar, was seated by his side. In the Address, after the usual complimentary sentiments and phrases, there was a reference to Bangalore's problems—the need for more roads, housing, water, civic amenities, etc., and above all, the need for more funds, for which the Minister's help was solicited. When it came to Shastriji's turn to reply, he thanked them for the honour done to him. Then he went on to say: "You have referred to some of your problems, with which I am in full sympathy. But why have you addressed them to me, because I am only a Minister without Portfolio? At one time I was the Home Minister of India, and I thought I was a big and powerful man. But, along came a man called Mr. Kamaraj, and he said, 'I have a Plan'. As a result of that Kamaraj Plan, I found office and power vanishing away from me. However, constituted as I am, I accepted this change without getting upset, and was settling down to my befitting role of a quiet, constructive worker. But suddenly Panditji fell gravely ill at Bhubaneshwar, and then along came this man, Mr. Kamaraj, once again and told me. "You have got to help Panditji". So he took me by the ear and brought me back into the Cabinet, though this time as a Minister without Portfolio. So you see (pointing to Shri Kamaraj), this is where the real power resides. So why not address your problems to him?"

More seriously however, he outlined his philosophy and approach to life in a letter dated 6th October 1963 sent to me in London. After four and half gruelling years with him I had managed to get away to the U.K. on a Nuffied Foundation Fellowship in May 1963. Shortly thereafter came his resignation from the post of Home Minister under the Kamaraj Plan. Knowing full well his family circumstances and the difficulties he must have been facing. I had written a very feeling letter to him. In reply to that came this intensely moving letter of October 1963, which, so far as I know, is the only expression in writing he ever made of his general philosophy and approach to life. The original is in his simple and highly effective Hindi, which is given in Appendix, and is well worth going through. I have attempted a translation in English, which is as follows:

LAL BAHADUR SHASTRI

1, York Place
New Delhi
October 6, 1963

My dear Rajeshwar Prasadji

Namaskar. I had received your letter of the 2nd

September, and yesterday I also received your letter of the 28th September. I am sorry I could not write to you earlier. I have been extremely busy during the last one month. There was the election of the new Chief Ministers and the formation of their Cabinets etc. and these took a great deal of time. We have not yet been able to resolve the disputes in Uttar Pradesh. The situation there is causing concern. Our colleagues in U.P. do not seem to realize how much harm they are causing to the State. They are so pre-occupied with their individual rivalries.

Panditji wanted very much that I should continue on my post. He mentioned this several times, but I myself wished to leave office. I had always been feeling uncomfortable in my mind about giving advice to others and not acting upon it myself. The speed with which we in the Congress are going down is sometimes frightening. Government administration in the districts is rapidly reaching a low level. No strong opposition party has been able to emerge. In these circumstances if some of us in Government come out and do something, then this relinquishing of office should be welcomed.

So far the signs are not very favourable. But it is hardly surprising that such a big step should give rise to some doubts and hesitations in the beginning. For those of us who are regarded as experienced and elders, this is a testing time. I feel that the fault is ours and not that of our Congress workers in the states or the districts. The next few months will show just how much utility we will have outside. I am not without hope.

Difficulties and hardships in the household will have to be put up with. A person learns to adjust himself. I have not yet shifted from my house but I shall be going to a smaller house. We have reduced one vegetable dish, as well as milk, and have started washing some of our clothes ourselves. I am using Ramji's[1] car and shall put in the petrol myself. We shall have to be careful in respect of other things also. I have left office twice before also and

1. Shastriji's younger son-in-law, Shri Vijay Nath Singh.

this is the third time. This time there are a few more facilities than on the previous occasions. Hari[2] is also now employed. There is also the Parliament allowance. It is, however, a fact that the burden of expenditure has greatly increased. The truth is that the help and co-operation of my wife is most sincere and without parallel, and I get great strength and support from her. So we shall manage somehow. It is natural for you to be concerned. It is perhaps better not to think too much about what may come. I believe that whatever HE does, we should accept accept cheerfully.

Hariye na himmat, bisariye na Ram ko
Jahi vidhi rakhen Ram, Tahi vidhi rahiye

Do not lose heart and forsake Ram.
In whatever manner HE chooses to keep you
in that manner should you learn to live.

On the 2nd of October, all of us went to Rajghat. It was the same familiar scene except the new constructions which had come up around the Samadhi. The memory of Gandhiji brings one close to tears. All of us are consumed by the desire for comfort and office. The feeling of service and dedication is so much less evident in office. Gandhiji's renunication was utter and complete. The story of his life is summed up in the beautiful verse of Kabir:

Das Kabir jatan se odhi, Jyon ki tyon dhar
deeni Chadariya[3]

Thy servant Kabir used this coverlet with
care and left it just as he found it

At Rajghat Panditji recollected that it was my birth-day also. The conversation which took place has been reported

2. Shri Hari Krishna Shastri, the eldest son.
3. *Chadariya* is a coverlet; the mortal frame is compared to a coverlet by Sant Kabir, who was a weaver by profession.

in *Navbharat* as follows:

Gandhi's birthday is everyone's birthday

New Delhi, 2nd October: This morning at Rajghat, Shri Nehru asked Shastriji "I hear that today is your birthday?" Shastriji, who does not ordinarily make any mention of this fact, replied, "Today is the birthday of Gandhiji, and hence it is not only mine but everyone's birthday."

I am glad to know that you and your wife are keeping good health and are happy. You will come back with new experience and new knowledge. You will be of even greater utility to Government and to the country. I am sure that you would have put every moment to the best possible use. I would like to convey, even at this stage, the congratulations and felicitations of all of us.

Ajay, Alok, Ravi and Anshu[4] are all well. They came here and had their meals with us on two occasions. We also met them when we went to Maheshwar Prasadji's[5] house for dinner. They are all living happily, although they must be missing you both and looking eagerly forward to your return. You and perhaps more than you, your wife, must also be longing to see them again. She must be wondering why the date for return does not come sooner.

I met your elder brother[6] also. Maheshwar Prasadji is still in the Home Ministry.

All else is well.

Yours
(Sd.) Lal Bahadur

Shri Rajeshwar Prasad, IAS
7, Prince Albert Road
London, NW-I

4. The 3 sons and daughter of Shri Rajeshwar Prasad.
5. Shri Maheshwar Prasad, IAS, younger brother of Shri Rajeshwar Prasad, who took his place as Special Assistant to the Home Minister.
6. Shri Rameshwar Prasad, I.C.S.

CHAPTER 3

ENDEARING QUALITIES

ONE OF Lal Bahadurji's most endearing characteristics was his utter simplicity—simplicity in thought, word and deed. This used to be exemplified in his dress itself. There is a humorous and endearing example of this. Once the closed collar black coat of 'pattu' that he used to wear on formal occasions had got so worn out that even the weave was becoming visible. To replace it the family got a black pashmina coat made to the measure of the old coat. But when Shastriji was shown this, he reacted sharply and firmly refused to wear anything so bright and shining. Since he was going to Calcutta to attend an important dinner where the Prime Minister (Pt. Nehru) would be present, the old pattu coat, all mussed up at the tailor's, was hurriedly got dry-cleaned, and both the coats were put into his suitcase and sent off to Calcutta. When the time for the dinner came, Shastriji put on his old coat, but having just come from the dry cleaner's it had a very strong, almost unbearable odour. Seeing his desperation we persuaded him to lay it aside, and put on the new black pashmina coat for just this once, which he reluctantly did. But all the way in the car he kept saying. "These people (the home people) act so thoughtlessly (*Nasamjhi se*) and get this sort of coat prepared for me. What will people say when they see me wearing this *chamkili, bharkili* (shining, exotic) dress. So I will go quietly to some corner of the hall and try to be as inconspicuous as possible." But the moment he entered the hall, the first person he ran into was none other than Pt. Jawaharlalji himself. Panditji took a good look at him, and then placing his hands on both shoulders brought Shastrji into the light, and then gave him a big whack on the back and said, "Lal Bahadur, you are wearing pashmina. Now you are becoming fashionable." Shastriji, who looked as if he was praying that the Earth would open up and swallow him, was just able to mumble: "Ji, I did not wear it. She (meaning Smt. Shastri) put it in my suitcase." Upon which Panditji gave him another whack on the back and said: "Well, one day she will put a pair of *paijamas* in your suitcase, and then you can start wearing *paijamas* also".

But Shastriji would never agree to wear *paijamas*, so wedded was he to his *dhoti*. The only occasion when he did wear them was at the Rashtrapati-Bhavan dinner in honour of the Queen of England in 1961, when his daughters, who were keen on getting a first-hand account of the glamorous young queen, virtually lifted and put him into a pair of *churidar paijamas* to attend the Rashtrapati Bhavan formal dinner.

Even when he was the Minister for Commerce and Industry, when there was not only the opportunity but also the necessity for the Minister to go abroad, Shastriji would avoid going, because he did not want to wear anything other than the dhoti. It was in vain that I kept trying to persuade him to make some foreign visits, because if he went then I could go too. But Shastriji used to say that it would be difficult to manage abroad wearing a dhoti, and he would not wear anything else. When I pointed out that Gandhiji used to go abroad in a loin cloth, he said that Gandhiji's case was quite different, he was in a class by himself; but he himself would rather forego the foreign visits than give up his *dhoti*. And so in the giant Ministry of Commerce & Industry with unlimited opportunities for foreign travel, I used to gnash my teeth in impotent rage and keep putting up to the Minister almost daily files for clearance of officers going abroad to all the five continents and seven seas, while the head of the Ministry himself was unwilling to stir a foot outside India. It was only much later, after he became Prime Minister and could go anywhere in his *dhoti*, that Shastriji began to experience the pleasures of travel abroad.

This simplicity in dress used to communicate itself to us, who worked in close proximity to him. One felt very uncomfortable wearing a suit and tie before him. Not that he would ever say anything, unlike some others, for instance Pt. Govind Ballabh Pant. When Pantji was Chief Minister, U.P. after Independence he had been invited by the U.P. ICS-IAS Association to address their annual gathering. Pantji, his head and hand shaking owing to his ailment, looked around the room with all the officers in their best suits and colourful ties, and his first remark was: "*Desh ke sare bandhan khul gaye, kintu aap logon ke gale ka bandhan nahin khul paya*". (The country has been freed of all its bonds, but the bond around your necks still remains.) Shastriji would never dream of making any such remark, but his love of utter simplicity spoke for itself. I still remember one particular occasion when I felt acutely embarrassed. My wife, Aruna, who until that time had not given up her hopes of making a colourful personality out of so colourless a person as myself, thought that what I lacked in internal sparkle could be made up by external colouring. Amongst some clothes she had got prepared for me was a very bright blue dressing gown with some striking motif on it, which may have resembled flowers or even stars. So eye-catching was it that I was careful never to wear it in Shastriji's presence. But once when on tour with him, I was woken up around midnight by the Minister's PA who said that the Minister was working in the next room and wanted me in connection with a certain file. I was wearing a *paijama* suit, and it would have taken too much time to get dressed all over again; so rather reluctantly I put on my bright blue dressing gown, flowers and all, and went into his room. He was looking towards the door, and at the sight of the apparition which entered, he gave a start as if something had struck him between the eyes. Yet, thereafter, he said not a word: but whenever he looked at me, a faint smile kept playing on his lips, and I could hardly have felt more embarrassed had I gone there in the nude.

Another of his lovable characteristics was his courtesy and consideration for others. This is something that knew no bounds, and the greatest as well as the humblest felt completely at home with him. One had only to meet him to succumb to his charm.

I recall my own first meeting with him on the 11th January 1959, when he was the Minister in charge of the then giant Ministry of Commerce and Industry, and I had come to take over as his Private Secretary. I hardly knew him at all, because the only occasion I had come into contact with him was when I was District Magistrate, Etawah in U.P. in 1955-56, and he had come on a brief one-day unofficial visit as Railway Minister. I had just received him at the Railway Station in the morning and seen him off at night. And now, at the instance of the then Chief Secretary, U.P., Shri Govind Narain, I was coming to work in such close proximity to him. Shri Govind Narain as Home Secretary, U.P. had worked closely with Shastriji when he was the Police Minister, and at the latter's request to send him an officer in whom he could have the utmost confidence, he (Shri Govind Narain) overcame my reluctance and persuaded me to go. Shastriji was already one of the big names in the Congress and the Government, and I could not help feeling a little nervous and wondering how I should conduct myself, and how I should thank him for reposing so much confidence in me, and so on. But the moment I entered his spacious room in Udyog Bhavan, the Minister rose from his seat, walked round the table and came up to me, and shook hands warmly. Before I could get in a word to thank him, he thanked me for having agreed to work with him. I was left dumbfounded at the transparent modesty and innate courtesy of so big a man.

That this was not a one-time show, but was something deeply inherent in his character and personality, I saw for myself times without number during the seven years that I worked with him. In all that period I can scarcely recall an abrupt or peremptory order from him like "Do this" or "Don't do that". It was generally in a question form, or a gentle hint upon which you had to act. For instance, when going on tour he used to say something like: "I am going next week to Calcutta, would you like to come along?" Now the relationship of the Minister and his Special Assistant is like the relationship of Mary and her little lamb: "Everywhere that Mary went the lamb was sure to go". So there was never any question of liking or disliking; it was just the Minister's gentle way of putting it. But lest there be any misunderstanding that this was an indication of softness on his part, I shall recount later how this gentle phrase was more in the nature of a commandment written on stone.

Likewise, whenever he had to call me to his residence late at night or very early in the morning, the phraseology used to be something like this: 'If it is not too much trouble, could you come over at 6 a.m.? or "If it is not inconvenient, could you stay on a little late and finish the draft"? Most of the time the remark *was in question form*, and the burden of proof was entirely on you, to say that it was no trouble at all, or that there was no question of any inconvenience. Once, when I had worked on an important draft speech at his residence till about 2 a.m., I completed it and laid it on his table, and coming home I told my wife that the meeting in Vigyan Bhavan is only at 10 a.m. So please do not wake me before 9 a.m. But the next morning she shook me awake at 6 a.m. and when I protested, she whispered: "What am I to do? The Minister is sitting just outside in the verandah". This was one of those small D-II Meena Bagh flats where the bedroom door opened out into the small front verandah. I jumped out of bed and rushed out—albeit this time without my blue-flowered dressing gown—to see the Minister sitting patiently in the verandah. On seeing me, he remarked: "I am sorry to disturb you again so early in the morning when you were sitting up till so late last night. But there are one or two important points that I wanted to clarify. Since it would have been too much trouble for you to come again so early, I have come over myself." What could one say to a man like that?

When he was Home Minister he used to sit at his semi-circular table in South Block, where there was room at the table for only one chair—his own. I used to stand alongside and help him with the files. Generally, this used to be quite late at night, after 10 p.m. or so. After sometime he used to say: "You also sit down". Where was I to squeeze in a chair for myself at that semi-circular table? So I would say: "I have been sitting all day and am tired of sitting. I would like to stand for a while". He would resume his perusal of the files, and then suddenly he would push back his chair and say: "I am also tired of sitting. Let me also stand for a while". And so with both of us standing at the Home Minister's table, we would continue looking through the files.

This same extraordinary courtesy and consideration was displayed when we went on tour. On reaching the Raj Bhavan concerned I would go to his room to see whether everything was as he would like it. And then to my amazement I would find that he had gone to my room to have a look at it. He would tell the Raj Bhavan staff. "Please do not mistake him for a PA. He is a senior IAS Officer of U.P. who has done me a favour by coming to work with me" (*Mere' yahan aakar mujh par inayat ki hai*). The richness of the Urdu word can scarcely be matched in English. He used to keep telling his PAs: "I am a Minister and there are so many people to look after me. You should take care of the SA. "*Voh bahut sankochi jeev hain, muh se kuch bolte nahin par mahsoos bahut karte hain*" (he is a somewhat shy and reticent being who does not speak out but feels things deeply)—which is perhaps correct. Thus even on these tours I would sometimes ask myself in bewilderment whether I was supposed to look after him, or he was supposed to look after me.

Another instance of his extreme consideration is that which he extended to my wife Aruna. In 1960 she and I had gone on a pilgrimage to Gangotri, which included several days of trekking on foot, and I had also managed to cover the difficult and at that time dangerous route to Gomukh, the real source of the Ganga, from where I had brought back a little of the sacred water. Shastriji had been camping at that time in Dehra Dun, which is my home, and had seen us off at the start of the trek. When we returned Aruna brought some of the holy Ganga water of Gangotri and Gomukh to Smt. Lalita Shastri. She also mentioned in Shastriji's presence that now her dearest wish was to offer some of these sacred waters from the high Himalayas at the shrine of Rameswaram washed by the southern seas. Shastriji remarked that when she had already covered the difficult part where no road or proper communication facilities existed, going to Rameswaram, which was well connected by rail and road, should be a much simpler matter. But in view of the extreme distance involved, Aruna did not cherish much hope of being able to fulfil her ambition early. Imagine her surprise and joy, when a few months later Shastriji sent word to her that he was flying to Madurai to attend the Southern Zonal Council Meeting at Kanya Kumari, and she should come along with him in the special plane to Madurai, from where he would arrange for her onward journey to Rameswaram. Hers had been a chance remark about offering the water of these Himalayan shrines in the great temple of the far South, but Shastriji had kept it in mind and at the first opportunity, he took the initiative in helping her to bring her dream to fruition.

One of the qualities Shastriji will always be remembered for was his humility. He was in every sense of the word an Apostle *of Humility*, and he remained so till the end even as Prime Minister. There is a great sweetness as well as strength in humility, and Shastriji's humility was one of the sources of his strength. He used to say that from childhood he was attracted by one of the verses of Guru Nanak Dev: "*Nanak, nanhe hi raho, jaise nanhi doob, Aur rukh sookh jayenge, doob khoob ki khoob*" (Nanak, be small like the little blade of grass: When the other trees wither and die, the grass will continue to remain green).

I could cite innumerable instances of his humility, but perhaps just one or two will suffice. Once as Home Minister he was in Calcutta and had to catch the flight back to Delhi. It was the evening rush hour, and there was little hope of his completing the long drive to Dum Dum Airport in time to catch the plane to Delhi. The Commissioner of Police said that he would send a pilot car with a siren ahead, so that the Minister could have a clear road. But Shastriji immediately and firmly declined. When some one expostulated, Shastriji said that the Police car would go ahead making a loud noise with the siren, and everyone would think that some big man was driving down, and then they would feel let down to see what "thing" had come along—*Kya cheez chali aiyee hai.*

On another occasion, as Prime Minister, he was to visit one of the States, but at the last minute he found it difficult to get away. So he rang up the Chief Minister and begged of him to excuse him (PM). But the Chief Minister was naturally cut up, and he pleaded with Shastriji: "Please do not disappoint us. I have made really first class arrangements for your visit". To which Shastriji's instinctive response on the spur of the moment was: "Why do you make first class arrangements for a third class person"?

Perhaps the most touching tribute of all to his humility was by the guard at the gate when his dead body lay in State at 10, Janpath on that cruel night of 11th January 1966. Thousands of people were filing past in silent and tearful tribute, and the guards at the gate had been instructed to see that everyone came in line in single file. But it was observed that people were breaking the line and coming out of turn, and that was causing commotion and confusion. So I went along with the PM's security-in-charge, Shri G.C. Dutt, a Joint Director of the Intelligence Bureau, to the gate, and the Security Chief pulled up the guard for allowing people to come out of turn and break the line. I still remember his reply: "Sir, what can I do? I keep begging them with folded hands not to break the line, but they keep saying 'Who are you to stop me? Don't you know, I am so and so', and insist on going in then and there. The only thing I know is that he whom they have all come to see, if he had come here I would have had no hesitation in stopping him, and I know that he would have had no hesitation in listening to me." That tribute from the guard at the gate while Shastriji's dead body lay in State was perhaps the most touching tribute of all.

Those of us who worked closely with him will always remember his forgiveness and magnanimity. There were times when we could not help playing truant. On tours with the Minister, one would accompany him in a car to a function. The moment he got out he would be garlanded and photographed, while we slunk out of the other door. On entering the hall there would be more clapping, more garlanding, more photographing, while the Minister was led to the seat of honour on the dais. But since the Minister was the last to arrive, by the time we entered with him, every single seat would be occupied, and there was no place to seat ourselves. And while we were circling round and round, trying desperately to find some place to park ourselves, we would see businessmen jump up when they saw some local officer such as the Deputy Chief Controller, Imports and Exports, and rush to offer him their seats, at the same time shouting for paan and cigarettes and cold drinks for the Deputy Chief Sahib. After sometime, all this used to get on our nerves, and when we felt we had enough we would just take a car and vanish from the scene and proceed on some outing. Later at night we would tiptoe to his room. If he was in good humour he would smile and ask whether we had been able to see everything (*Aap log sab kuch dekh dakh aye*)—and then we knew we were forgiven, and we would launch into enthusiastic descriptions of the places we had visited, and urge him to find some time to go there himself (which seldom was the case). But at other times when he was not in so good a mood, he would take a deep breach and say "*Accha aap log ghoom gham aye hain*" (so you have been roaming about). Not a word more would he utter in reproach or recrimination, but we used to slink away with our tails between our legs.

An outstanding example of his magnanimity relates to a

period before I joined him, when he was Minister for Transport and Civil Aviation. The turbo-prop Viscount Aircraft, with pressurized interior, had just been acquired for Indian Airlines, and a special flight had been arranged over the Himalayan regions of Kumaon and Garhwal. Shastriji had invited the Prime Minister for the flight, and he was looking forward eagerly to having a few hours alone with the PM in a relaxed mood, as well as seeing the scenic beauty of the snow mountains and glaciers.

On the evening before the flight, he asked his then Private Secretary, an IAS Officer of the U.P. Cadre, whether the flight would be from the Palam Airfield. But the Private Secretary said that he had checked up, and the flight would take off from Safdarjang Airport. Shastriji expressed surprise because he had been told that this aircraft needed a longer runway, but he said that it was just as well that it was taking off from Safdarjang, because it would save the time involved in the long drive to Palam.

Early the next morning the Private Secretary had hardly got up when he received a phone call from the Minister's residence asking whether he could come over. He was greatly shocked to learn that the Minister was still at home, and inquired whether he had not gone for the Special Flight with the PM. The PA said that he had got ready and gone out but returned after sometime, and was now going through the files, in which connection he had asked for the PS.

My predecessor rushed to Shastriji's residence in a puzzled state of mind, and asked him why he had not gone for the special flight, to which he had been looking forward so much. Shastriji replied that he had gone, but as advised yesterday, he had gone to Safdarjang Airport, only to learn that the flight was from Palam. At this stage if he had now to go all the way to Palam, he would be quite late in reaching, and this would have annoyed the Prime Minister, who was a stickler for punctuality. As Shastriji jokingly put it: "He would have told me in front of everybody; 'Lal Bahadur, you are still living in the 16th century'. So rather than going back to the 16th century, I decided to come back home, after sending a telephone message to Palam expressing regrets and pleading to be excused on the ground of feeling unwell".

Knowing how much Shastriji had looked forward to this flight over the snow mountains and the opportunity of being alone with the PM, my predecessor was filled with shame and remorse at his careless mistake, and told the Minister that he did not know how to even ask for forgiveness. To which the Minister replied that the flight would have taken up several hours, whereas now he had the whole of the early morning to get through his files. So he said: "Let us not waste any more time. You just sit down and let us get on with our work". A more supreme example of magnanimity it is difficult to imagine.

One of his most notable characteristics was his shining integrity, which shines out all the more in the murkiness and gloom of the venality of present-day politics. Although Shastriji was so close to Jawaharlalji, who did so much to build him up, yet in spirit he was much closer to Gandhiji, whom he revered. Like Gandhiji his personal life was characterized by ascetism and austerity, with a supreme disdain for worldly pleasures and the riches that money could bring.

He himself never handled money. At home his wife took care of all the requirements, and on tour his PAs used to do the tipping in Raj Bhavans etc, and handle any matters where money was required. Perhaps if Shastriji had been shown a ten rupee note and a five rupee note from a distance, he would not have been able to tell which was which.

It is surely a matter for inspiration and pride that one who held the supreme post of Prime Minister of India, when he passed away he had no house of his own, not an inch of land to his name, and he left behind only instalments of a Government loan taken for purchase of a car. As one of his sons has aptly remarked. "Our father did not leave any wealth or posessions, only his name and fame. Why then should we not benefit from the same"? This austerity of renunication, it is this which has inspired Indians throughout the ages, where saints and sages have always taken a higher place than kings and conquerors. Shastriji in his own life lived upto the high ideal of his favourite Bhajan of Sant Kabir: *Das Kabir jatan se odhi, Jyon ki tyon dhar deeni Chadariya.*

Shastriji's veneration for Gandhiji has already been brought out in the letter to me in London reproduced earlier. Gandhiji himself used to remark that while Jawaharlal was the uncrowned king of India, nothing would give him greater happiness than if a Kisan were to hold the topmost post in India, Shastriji was not a kisan, but he belonged to the same strata of society, and had known appalling poverty in his early life. One likes to think that in his ascedancy to the Prime Ministership, Gandhiji's dearest wish had come true, and that the Mahatma's spirit in Heaven must have rejoiced.

There are some coincidental resemblances also. Both Gandhiji and Shastriji shared a common birthday—the 2nd of October. Both passed away in the same month—January. And while Shastriji did not share the Mahatma's martyrdom, there was the same abrupt, shocking and heart-breaking end. Gandhiji had lived a full life. His last months were filled with disillusionment, but the country very much needed his guidance and soothing touch in the turbulent infancy of independence. Shastriji passed away at the height of his power and glory, when his countrymen and the world were looking forward to so much more from him. In the case of both Gandhiji and Shastriji had the cruel hand of Death not snatched them away when it did, the history of this country might have been very different.

CHAPTER 4

THE GREAT CONCILIATOR

LAL BAHADURJI acquired a name for himself by his skill as a negotiator. That is why Pandit Jawaharlal Nehru kept entrusting the most difficult and delicate negotiations to him. One of the secrets of his extraordinary success as a negotiator was his ability to see the other man's point of view. He was always ready to make the maximum allowance for the other person's feelings. There were times when one wished he were a little firmer, but the success of his methods was its own answer.

I recollect one striking example of this understanding and making allowance for the other man's point of view. When he was Minister of Commerce and Industry, he accepted the invitation of one of the Chambers of Commerce in Calcutta to address an important function of theirs. The practice on such occasions is that the draft speech of the Chamber's President is sent beforehand, on the basis of which the Ministry suggests the draft of the Minister's address. In this case when the draft speech of the President was received, it was found to be a scathing criticism of the Government's policies and the Ministry's functioning, and there were also untoward remarks about the Minister himself. On seeing this draft, the Secretary of the Ministry, Shri S. Ranganathan (later the Comptroller and Auditor General) sent for me. He was flanked by the two Additional Secretaries in charge of Industry and Commerce, Shri L.K. Jha and Shri K.B. Lall. The Secretary said that having invited the Minister, it was very unbecoming of the Chamber's President to launch this tirade against the Government, and that too with so much vituperation. So he wanted me to ensure that the Minister gave a fitting and forceful reply. I pointed out that it would not be easy to get the Minister to say anything forceful, but the Secretary said that it was not just a personal matter but official policy was involved, and a firm reply must be given. Knowing the Minister's nature, I toned down the Ministry's draft as much as possible, but left a few strong sentences here and there.

On the flight to Calcutta, the Minister as usual took off his cap and his shoes, put on his spectacles and took up his pencil (he preferred to work in pencil on his drafts). In fact, this is one of the postures in which I best remember him. He took out the draft speech prepared for him, went through it carefully, and one by one cut out all the sentences that smacked of firmness. I remonstrated and mentioned to him what the Secretary had told me about giving a firm and forceful reply in view of the very unbecoming and vituperative speech of the Chamber President. To this Lal Bahadurji replied. "If something must be said forcefully, then it should be. But in that case you should find another Minister to say it, because I cannot say anything harshly to anybody". I again pleaded with him and emphasized how unworthy was the conduct of the President in first inviting and then virtually abusing the Minister. But Shastriji just smiled and said, "You are all big officers. When you sit behind your big tables in your big offices, you forget the trials and sorrows of the common people. But I am one of them. How can I be blind to their trials and tribulations? "This President" he said, "Do you think he is mad that he should have spat poison in this manner? Times without number he must have tramped the corridors of Udyog Bhavan, knocking at door after door, but all in vain. And thus, driven to despair and desperation, he has given vent to his feelings of exasperation. How can I be annoyed with him? Rather, I should take pity on him". What could I say thereafter?

However, when the meeting commenced, we hoped that in the presence of the Minister the President would have the good sense to tone down his speech. But he was a young man of about 35, and he read out all that he had written with great vehemence, and with a curl of the lip and a sneer. There was a hush when the Minister rose to reply. But Shastriji just said quietly, "Your President has spoken with great fire and fury. He is a young man, but I am an old man. How can I hope to find such fire and fury in myself? So I will not attempt to emulate him, but shall confine myself to giving you the facts". Upon which, he proceeded to read out his speech in an even tone, and in his usual calm and dignified manner. And no sooner had he finished than we saw the amazing spectacle of Member after Member of that Chamber of Commerce getting up and apologizing to the Minister and repudiating their President, who sat at the head of the table looking thoroughly downcast with his face almost buried in his hands.

Likewise, Lal Bahadurji had it in him to give a gentle but quite effective rebuff when called for, but without wounding the other person's feelings. As Minister of Commerce & Industry, he had to decide on the location of the Heavy Electrical Plants which were to come up with Soviet aid. As usual, there was a clamour from many of the States for siting of one plant out of these in their territory. Shastriji set up a Technical Committee to make a thorough study and put up recommendations. It was presided over by a retired Chairman of the Railway Board, a very competent person, but one with such exalted notions of himself that his hat would perhaps not be able to sit on his swollen head. Once, when the Minister was flying to Hyderabad, the Chairman and the members of the Technical Committee were on the same plane with him. Those days the planes used to be the 44 seater pressurized Turbo-prop Viscounts, so that it was hardly possible for the passengers to avoid noticing one another. We were therefore shocked when the Chairman and Members passed the Minister without a word of greeting. We told Shastriji it was you who appointed the members of this Committee and gave them this opportunity after retirement, and yet they do not even wish to greet you. But Shastriji just smiled and made no reply.

That afternoon there was a big public meeting in Hyderabad. The Chairman and Members of the Technical Committee were also present. The Chief Minister, Shri Brahmananda Reddy, in his speech told Shastriji that Hyderabad was making available the land, water, power, etc., for a Heavy Electrical Plant, and requested, amid appalause, that Shastriji should kindly see to it that it was given to Hyderabad. When it was his turn to reply, Shastriji said that he would personally be very happy if Hyderabad got one of the Heavy Electrical Units. But these things, he said, had to be decided on a number of economic and technical considerations, and so he had appointed a Technical Committee to examine all aspects and make recommendations.

And he said "You can be very sure that theirs would be a thoroughly objective and impartial report. And how objective it is going to be you can judge from this, that although the Chairman and the Members travelled down on the same plane with me this morning, they took care to avoid greeting me, lest I influence them in your favour". In the burst of laughter that followed, the faces of the Chairman and his colleagues were worth seeing.

One of his greatest qualities was his extraordinary patience. Even the proverbial patience of Job could hardly have matched his own. He had an infinite capacity for listening and bearing up. And this was one of the main factors behind his great achievements in trouble-shooting. Of trouble-shooters it has been aptly said that whether or not they are able to shoot that particular trouble, one only hopes that they will not succeed in creating more trouble elsewhere. But that was not the case with Shastriji, because his trouble-shooting consisted entirely of bringing to bear the healing touch. And he was able to do so, because of his infinite patience in listening to the other person's grievances, than which few things can be more soothing to wounded feelings. This was the quality he displayed in all the difficult situations he faced, and which he successfully resolved: Cachar and the Sangram Parishad Movement, the Assam Language Disturbances, Kerala and the power struggle between warring Ministers, Nepal—smoothing the ruffled feathers of the King of Nepal, the Akali Agitation and Master Tara Singh's Fast, and the Hazratbal Sacred Relic tension in Kashmir.

Soon after taking over as Home Minister in March 1961 he was faced with the Assam Language problem and the explosive situation in the Bengali-speaking Cachar district over what they considered to be imposition on them of the Assamese language. There had been Police firing in Silchar and a number of deaths, and feelings were running high when the Home Minister came to Cachar. All the way from the banks of the Barak river to the district headquarters at Silchar, there were young boys and girls standing on either side of the road absolutely silent, but with placards of protest in their hands. It was a most effective and telling silent demonstration. And at the Circuit House in Silchar, the leaders of the Movement waited to give vent to their pent-up feelings. But they waited in vain. For the Home Minister first visited the Hospital and spoke to those who had been wounded in the Police firing. Then he went to the Jail and met some of those who had been imprisoned. He even managed to meet and speak a few words of grief and sympathy to relatives of some of those killed in the firing. And it was quite late at night when he finally landed up at the Circuit House, by which time many of those assembled had dispersed, and the feelings of bitterness and animosity had been considerably dispelled.

One of the finest examples of how patience was Shastriji's source of strength was his handling of the difficult situation in Kerala as Home Minister. Serious differences had arisen between the Praja Socialist Party Chief Minister, Shri Pattom Thannu Pillai and the Congress Deputy Chief Minister Shri R. Sankar, which endangered the working of the Coalition Cabinet. The Prime Minister deputed Shastriji to resolve the deadlock.

For a whole day and well into the night Shastriji sat in the Raj Bhavan in Trivandrum meeting scores of people, one after the other. It was an exhausting process, and because he sat we had no option save to keep sitting too. At the end of a tiring day Shri L.P. Singh, who was then Additional Secretary in the Home Ministry and had accompanied Shastriji to Kerala, said "Sir, you know the whole problem inside out. You know the lines on which a solution is to be attempted. So why not place it before them and have done with it, instead of listening to scores of people telling you the same things over and over again, and wearing you ragged in the process?" Shastriji just smiled and said, "You know the people here feel so strongly about these matters that it just keeps welling and bubbling within them. If I were to choke them off and say 'I know all about these matters, you just listen to me,' would they be in the mood to listen to what I say? Now you see what is happening. Each one comes and tells me 'Shastriji, you don't know this fellow. He is a rouge and should be put behind bars' and in the process he will bang the table. I just keep murmuring, 'O I never knew. Thank you so much for telling me'. And when he goes out his admirers are waiting for him in the lawns of Raj Bhavan, and they gather round eager to know what has transpired. And the leader will again bang the table and get a tremendous kick out of telling *them: I told the* Home Minister this and that and that and so on. When he has got all this steam off his chest and some of the bitterness out of his system, do you not think he will be in a better frame of mind to listen to me and consider my suggestions?" And Shri L.P. Singh smiled and shrugged and said "Sir, you know best."

And so for 3 days and almost 3 nights, Shastriji sat in the Raj Bhavan listening to virtually hundreds of people. It was a tremendous strain on him and perhaps even more on us. But on the 4th day having listened to everybody, when he finally put forward his suggestions they met with ready acceptance. It is another matter that the compromise did not last long and had ultimately to be resolved by sending Shri Pattom Thanu Pillai away from Kerala as a Governor.

One of Shastriji's great successes was his defusing of the very tense and bitter relations which had come about between India and Nepal. The relationship could hardly have been worse when he went to Kathmandu in March 1963. King Mahendra had reacted very unfavourably to Pandit Jawaharlal's criticism of his action in dismissing the popularly elected government in December 1960, and the relations between the two countries had grown steadily worse. Nepal even suspected India of encouraging those involved in the attempt on the King's life at Janakpur. Likewise, India felt very strongly about Nepal's giving permission to China to build the Kathmandu-Kodari Highway, which led from the Tibetan border to the Kingdom's capital. From there a motor link leading straight down to India existed in the shape of the Indian-built Tribhuvan Rajpath. In the wake of the Chinese aggression of October-November 1962, it was thought prudent to mend fences with the King of Nepal in order to lessen the growing Chinese influence. Naturally, no one appeared to be better suited to the task than Shastriji, the great conciliator.

In the course of his brief visit, Shastriji was able to built up an excellent rapport with the King himself, and with the Prime Minister Shri Tulsi Giri, and the Home Minister Shri Vishwa Bandhu Thapa. As usual with him, he listened patiently to all that they had to say. Having given them full opportunity of ventilating their grievances, he in his turn was listened to patiently, and he was able to convince them of India's basic goodwill and friendliness towards Nepal. Perhaps more than what he said, they were struck by his sincerity and humility, and were touched by his homeliness. As he himself said when addressing a gathering, this was his first ever visit outside India, and he was looking forward to the experience of seeing a foreign country. But in Nepal he felt so much at home that he never got the feeling of being out of his own country. Even his wife with her traditional orthodoxy and fastidiousness for religious ceremonials felt completely at one with the land of Lord Pashupatinath. Nepal for them instead of being an alien land proved to be a home away from home.

Shastriji visit was not able to prevent the construction of the Kathmandu-Kodari Highway, but it gave all who mattered in Nepal the feeling that there was someone high up in India who understood their point of view. Henceforward there was a much better understanding between the two countries, and a restoration of the friendliness, which was heightened still further when Shastriji took over as Prime Minister in the following year.

He once again displayed his extraordinary skill as a negotiator through his patient approach and willingness to hear the other side in the way he handled the extraordinarily explosive situation created in the Kashmir Valley by the Hazratbal Sacred Relic case. The Relic consisting of the Hair of the Prophet had been found missing from the Hazratbal shrine, and this gave rise to a passionate outcry among the local people. After some days the authorities recovered the Relic but the local populace demanded that it should be shown to them before they accepted it as genuine. This the authorities headed by none less than the Union Home Secretary and the Director of the Intelligence Bureau, who were camping in Srinagar for days on end, were not prepared to concede for fear that if the authencity of the Relic was denied by any representative group the Valley would go up in flames. The situation had become so explosive that the ailing Jawaharlalji asked Shastriji, who has just returned to the Cabinet as Minister without Portfolio a few days earlier, to proceed at once to Srinagar and settle the situation on the spot.

It was the end of January 1964, and a bitterly cold winter. Srinagar lay under a thick blanket of snow. Panditji was so good as to lend Shastriji his overcoat to face the bitter cold.

Shastriji started off as usual by meeting all the persons he could possibly meet and hearing them out. The most influential person at that time appeared to be Maulana Masoodi of the

National Conference (Sheikh Abdullah was still under detention and Bakshi Ghulam Mohammad who had been asked to resign under the Kamaraj Plan was very much a discredited person). From talks with Maulana Masoodi, Mirwaiz Maulvi Farooq and others, Shastriji felt that the public needed to be shown the Relic to convince them that it was genuine. He was fully aware of the risks involved, which were high-lighted by the Home Secretary and the Director, Intelligence Bureau, but he felt that there was no way out and the risk would have to be taken. Although he had not yet taken a decision, this view of his was not liked and was even resented by those in charge. It seemed to us at the time that the topmost Law Enforcement Officers of the Government of India were, in the closed confines of a snow-bound Srinagar, functioning very much like a nervous District Magistrate and Superintendent of Police.

One night in the dining room (Shastriji used to dine quietly in his own room) the Home Secretary, who had evidently partaken freely of the cup that cheers, suddenly told me "Your Minister has some sort of reputation for sorting out difficult problems". I said quietly, "Yes Sir." On which he remarked "If he wishes to preserve the reputation, then advise him to go back to Delhi by the first available plane tomorrow, and remind him to take you with him." To which I again quietly replied "Yes Sir." Although I did not convey this conversation to the Minister yet he soon came to know of it from the Assistant Private Secretary and the Personal Assistants, who were also at the dining table.

The next day Shastriji called the Home Secretary and the Director of the Intelligence Bureau to a meeting in his room. He told them that as a result of his talks with the local leaders, he was convinced that a showing (Deedar) of the Relic was essential. He was also aware of the reservations of the authorities, but he had decided that the risk had to be taken. The Prime Minister had authorized him to take on-the-spot decisions and he had decided on the 'Deedar' But if the Home Secretary and the DIB still felt apprehensive, they need not take the responsibility, and he would make the arrangements with the help of the younger officers. In that case he would advise them to go back to Delhi by the first available plane. They at once understood that the Minister had become aware of last night's remarks in the dining hall and sheepishly they agreed to carry out his instructions.

The occasion of the 'Deedar' in the Hazartbal Shrine next afternoon was one fraught with tension and anxiety. It was a cold, cloudy afternoon with snow all around, and the Mosque on the banks of the Dal Lake as well as the surrounding area was jam-packed with people. Excellent policing arrangements had been made by by batch-mate Shri Sushital Banerji (who died later as Defence Secretary), but the Police were very much in the background. Shastriji was there along with Maulana Masoodi and the other leaders. It was a tense moment, because if the recovered Relic was not accepted as genuine, bloodshed was inevitable. But the moment the Relic was put on display, Maulana Masoodi and others took a look at it, and then prostrated themselves on the floor before it. Those standing behind, and in the courtyard could hardly have seen the Relic at all, but the example of the leaders was sufficient for them and they also prostrated themselves on the cold ground with cries of joy and devotion. What had been a period of nerve-tingling suspense became an occasion of rejoicing and celebration. The Home Secretary and the DIB with broad smiles on their faces after many a long day paid tribute to Shastriji's sagacity, when they saw him off at the Airport later that evening.

These same qualities were exhibited by Shastriji in handling the Akali agitation led by Master Tara Singh, who had gone on a hunger strike. At that time Shastriji as Home Minister was staying in the newly constructed Guest House in Chashma Shahi in Srinagar Valley, where the Prime Minister was also expected. Master Tara Singh had gone on a fast unto death, and this was causing anxiety, because everybody knew what the consequences would be if the fast went on to the bitter end. When Shastriji expressed his concern about this, I well remember that one of the officers in the room remarked, "Why should we allow him to make a martyr of himself?" Shastriji said "What can we do if he keeps on fasting until death?" The officer replied, "Surely we can arrange for him to be fed even against his will." Shastriji's reaction was so sharp that it was the nearest I have seen him to anger: "What the British did not do to Gandhiji and the rest of us during the freedom struggle, you want us to do after Independence. They were also aware of the consequences if

Gandhiji had died during any of his numerous fasts, but never did they do him the indignity of trying to force-feed him. If a man is prepared to make the supreme sacrifice of his life for a cause he holds dear, who are we to trample on human dignity and inflict this sort of insult upon him?"

On return to Delhi, he took up once again his trump-card of long and detailed negotiations. The leaders talked and talked. In the end Master Tara Singh was forced by circumstances to give up his fast, and he had to atone by doing penance in the form of cleaning shoes and used utensils in the gurudwara.

Laughingly, we used to say amongst ourselves, "Woe betide the movement that gets involved in negotiations with Shastriji. While he engaged their representatives in interminable discussions and the leaders talked and talked, the strength of the Movement gradually ebbed away".

CHAPTER 5

SOUND COMMON SENSE: FEET ALWAYS ON THE GROUND

One of Shastriji's greatest assets was his sound common sense. He knew the common man's reactions to a nicety. This was his touchstone with which he weighed every policy and measure that came before him. Being a man of the people he shared in full their thoughts, their emotions, their sentiments, their aspirations.

Like Abraham Lincoln, he was in every sense of the word "A boy from the backwoods". And as such he retained his touch with reality, with practicality. His giant predecessor, an idealist and dreamer par excellence, was often regarded as having his head in the clouds. Shastriji's feet always remained solidly on earth. There were no flights of fancy, but a clear-headed touch with reality.

He brought this approach into dealing with policies in the limited time that ultimately became available to him. In the field of foreign policy he used to say that while it was good to be functioning as one of the leaders of the Non-Aligned Movement and the Third World, and playing a mediating and moderating role between the two opposing Super Power Blocs, yet the first essential was to improve India's relations with her own neighbours, almost all of whom regarded her with distrust and suspicion. So he made it one of the priorities of his foreign policy to improve relations with the neighbouring countries. This is not always easy. Even Jesus Christ said "Love thy neighbour as thyself", probably because the neighbour is frequently the most difficult person to love. But Shastriji resolved to make the attempt.

With Nepal I have already mentioned the rapport he had built up with the King and Government of Nepal, which he further consolidated during his visit as Prime Minister in April 1965 on the occasion of the inauguration of the Kosi Barrage. Irritants still remained, like the King's suspicion about India's sympathies for the banned Nepal National Congress, and India's unhappiness over the construction by the Chinese of the Kathmandu-Kodari Highway. But there was a great deal of understanding because of the personal equation with the King and the Nepalese Prime Minister that Shastriji had established.

With Sri Lanka he entered into serious discussions with the Prime Minister, Mrs Sirimavo Bandaranaike on the thorny question of citizenship to the Indian labour working on the plantations, and the repatriation of those who did not qualify. The understanding which they reached, which came to be known as the Shastri-Sirimavo Pact, did much to relieve the irritants in the relations between the two countries.

With Burma, Shastriji visited Rangoon in December 1965, along with his family, and established a cordial relationship with General Ne Win. Incidentally, this was the last of his foreign visits before the fateful trip to Taskhent and its tragic end.

Even with India's two antagonistic neighbours, Pakistan and China, Shastriji attempted to mend fences. On the way back from the Non-Aligned Summit held in Cairo in October 1964, he dropped down at Karachi for a few hours and met General Ayub Khan. Both of them reiterated their desire for a friendlier relationship, a desire that was to be completely frustrated by subsequent events.

Even in the relationship with China, Shastriji threw out a feeler in Parliament that the strained relationship should not continue indefinitely and some attempt should be made to settle the boundary dispute. But at that time in 1964 the bitter memories of the Chinese aggression of 1962 were so strong, that this met with strong criticism even from some of his own Party men, and the cautious person that he was, Shastriji decided not to raise the issue again and to wait for better times (which for him never came).

On the subject of economic development, he had in his very first speech as Prime Minister in June 1964 highlighted the need to contain the price rise, which was hitting all classes, more especially the middle class. For the same reason he was of the view that our Five Year Plans should be commensurate with our resources, and that there was no use of having grandiose plans, for which we should go about seeking foreign aid. He used to say that if I as a private citizen start living beyond my means, I would end up in a debtor's prison. I just cannot understand why as a nation we should have extravagant plans far beyond our resources, and then go round the world with a begging bowl. But despite his sound instinct, he allowed himself to be persuaded by his Secretary, Shri L.K. Jha, and other economists that it was necessary to plan big, and that there was no harm in a certain measure of deficit financing. But had he been spared for some more time, I am sure he would never have allowed the extent of imbalance which came to exist between our expenditure and our resources.

He was one who believed that the growing gap between precept and practice was responsible for many of the ills in the body politic and in administration. One should be prepared to practice what he preaches. It was because of his basic honesty that while recognizing the importance of Family Planning in the Indian context and giving it all support at the Governmental level, he refrained from himself talking about it publicly. As he used to put it: "With what face can I, as a father of six surviving children, go round telling people: "*Do ya teen bus*" (Two or three and no more).

Despite appearing so simple outwardly Shastriji was a very shrewd person. No person could have risen so high by mere goodness and simplicity. Few things were hidden from him, and he could look right through men and matters. But in order to avoid getting involved in controversy he often kept his knowledge to himself and assumed an attitude of simplicity, even wonderment. But sometimes when he felt that people were taking him too much for granted, then jokingly he would say, "Please do not misjudge me. I am not as innocent as I look". The then U.S. Ambassador to India, Dr. J.K. Galbraith, put it very effectively when he said, "There is more iron in his soul than appears on the surface". And Shastriji in a more serious mood defended himself:

"Some people say my policies are weak. My language and manner may be soft, but I assure you I am not weak. I have no weakness at heart. These were words that he proved to the hilt in the Indo-Pakistan crisis of 1965 and the War that followed.

Perhaps this mistaken assumption of Shastriji's simplicity in thinking and innocence was partly due to his extraordinary capacity to conceal his inner feelings and always present a calm and unperturbed appearance. No matter how strongly he felt about certain situations, he never allowed his feelings to surface, and he could keep them deep within himself. On one occasion when certain developments took place in the family, which were deeply upsetting, he was the one person who kept his cool and refused to get perturbed, though he was deeply concerned. Quietly, unobstrusively, he handled the situation in his tactful and gentle manner, until matters were sorted out to everyone's satisfaction.

How calmly and coolly he could take even the most disturbing developments, I shall indicate when dealing with the Indo-Pak tension over the Kutch developments during his Prime Ministership in the first half of 1965. It was an amazing display of iron self-control. The deepest upsets and sorrows he could keep to himself. That is why one can visualize the excruciating agony he must have been suffering on that fatal night of 10th/11th January 1966, when a few minutes before the end, he kept pacing restlessly in his room with his hands on his chest and with the exclamation "Hai Ram, hai Baap" escaping from his lips.

The quiet Stoicism with which he took joy and sorrow alike, was again very much in evidence in the aftermath of Pt. Jawaharlalji's death. The whole country was agog with speculation and anxiety as to who would be the next Prime Minister, and this was the subject of excited discussion in every nook and corner of the subcontinent. Shri Morarji Desai had already indicated his candidature—"thrown his hat into the ring" as Shri Kuldip Nayar reported it. But Shastriji, who stood the best chance of all, refused to announce himself as a candidate or take any overt steps towards his selection. Calm and collected as ever, he left matters to Shri Kamaraj, the Congress President, and his colleagues, and stayed aloof from all politicking. And when ultimately chosen to be the Prime Minister, he took this great honour with a quiet dignity and without any outward display of exultation. On the other hand, he felt humbled at the immensity of the task in succeeding one who was amongst the foremost of our generation. When addressing the Congress leaders in the Central Hall of Parliament after his election he said: "I tremble when I am reminded of the fact that I have to be in charge of this country and Parliament, which has been led by no less a person than Jawaharlal Nehru".

How well he could control his feelings, he displayed during the four months he functioned as Minister Without Portfolio from about the end of January 1964 till Panditji's death on 27th May that year. This was a real testing time for him. He had been brought back into the Cabinet to assist the Prime Minister who had been temporarily incapacitated by the stroke in Bhubaneshwar, but was designated as Minister without Portfolio, and in view of the opposition of Shri Gulzari Lal Nanda and Shri T.T. Krishnamachari given only the No. 4 rank in the Cabinet. As long as the P.M. was too unwell to attend to any work, Shastriji more or less held full charge of the Ministry of External Affairs and the Cabinet Secretariat. But as soon as Jawaharlalji was a little better and could attend to some items of work from his residence, the Secretaries often started going straight to him, discussing important matters and then recording his instructions on the files, which was the first that Shastriji came to know of them. The Minister of State in the Ministry of External Affairs, Smt. Lakshmi Menon, had also not taken kindly to the interposition of a Cabinet Minister between herself and the Prime Minister, and preferred either to decide matters on her own, and when that was not possible, to deal directly with the P.M. as soon as he was better. It was an impossible position for Shastriji, but loyal as ever to Panditji, he chose to suffer in silence. With Panditji's health obviously failing, there was also the gnawing uncertainity of what was going to happen after him. To add to his misery, Shastriji began to sense that Panditji would very much like that his daughter should take his place. This was an intensely unhappy period for Shastriji, but deeply disturbed inwardly, he maintained his outward composure. It was only once or twice, late at night, when he chose to unburden himself in strict confidence to those of us working closely with him, that he remarked in a deeply depressed mood that when Panditji desired so much that his daughter should succeed him, then why does he not say so and *put us all out of this* misery and uncertainty. It was this feeling of his which Shri Kuldip Nayar disclosed in his book *Between the*

Lines, though Shastriji himself would have been horrified had he dreamed that within a few months of his death his in-most thoughts would be emblazoned before the world. At least Shastriji was one who would never have challenged any such decision of Panditji. But, unlike what happened later, Jawaharlalji was too refined a character, too true a democrat, to impose any successor on the nation, and kept insisting that in a democratic set-up it was for the people to decide.

Shy and retiring by nature Shastriji shrank from personal publicity, even on occasions when it would have been fully justified. How far this could go can be illustrated by just one instance. As Prime Minister he had attended the Non-Aligned Summit in Cairo in October 1964, and during the period of the Conference he had been housed in the Nile Hilton Hotel by the banks of the river. Since he was a strict vegetarian with very simple tastes, the normal hotel fare did not suit him at all. Hence the U.A.R. Government had made special arrangements for his attendant, Shri Ram Nath, to prepare his simple fare in a corner of the hotel kitchen. At that time the Hilton Hotel chain was negotiating for setting up hotels in India, beginning with Bombay, and their move was viewed with apprehension by the local hoteliers. In an obvious attempt to discredit Hilton Hotels, a story was put out in a newspaper that the Hilton Hotel had submitted a huge Bill to the Prime Minister for blackening the ceiling and walls of his hotel room by cooking in that room on a stove. This was totally baseless, as nothing of the sort ever occurred. But apart from the Hilton Hotel, it depicted the Prime Minister of India in an unfavourable light, giving the impression that he was such a rustic that he needed to get cooking done on a stove in his room in an expensive and elaborately furnished hotel. In view of this, some of us, who had been with him in Cairo, requested his permission to put out a news item giving the correct facts. But to this Shastriji would not agree. He was emphatic that anything concering him personally should not appear in the Press, even if only to correct a wrong impression.

However, it must be recorded that as the months went on during his Premiership, he had begun to listen more and more to the advice of his Public Relations staff about the need for publicity and image-building. He did not shrink from publicity to the same extent as before, and had even begun to welcome it. This was one of the gradual changes that came about in his personality during his Prime Ministership.

CHAPTER 6

HE WAS, AFTER ALL, HUMAN

ONE OF the guiding factors of his life was the desire for compromise, for the middle way, the golden mean. He would go to extreme lengths in his search for a compromise. His innate caution, his reluctance to hurt anyone inclined him naturally to seek compromises. He disliked ever having to cut the Gordian knot. The result was that he often wore himself and his staff out in the process. Even when it was obvious that two parties to a dispute would never agree, and he had to decide, he would ask us to go and meet one party and try to bring him around. When we reported failure, he would still suggest that we go and meet the other party. On being informed that that party too was adamant, he would express distress as well as a little annoyance and say that people insist on fighting like cats and dogs and want him to find a way out. It was with extreme reluctance that he would then settle down to take a decision, but the saving grace was that once he decided, he would not swerve from it.

One instance of his trying to help people even at the cost of attracting criticism to himself came when a former ICS Defence Secretary applied for permission to take up lucrative private employment very shortly after retirement. There had been a number of cases of Senior ICS Officers taking up such employment soon after retirement, and there had been strong criticism about this in Parliament and the Press. So much so, that Shastriji as Home Minister had stated on the floor of the Lok Sabha that Government was concerned about this tendency and had decided that no such permission would be given hereafter. But when the case of this retired Defence Secretary, whom Shastriji knew well, came up, he kept looking through the file and wondering whether something could be done to help the officer. I told him that after his categorical statement in Parliament, there was no way out, and he should refuse the permission. He kept silent for some time and then said quietly: "*Aap inhee ko bali ka bakra banana chahatey hain* (you want to make him the sacrificial goat). Only some time back Panditji gave permission to so and so, while Krishna Menon benefited such and such an officer, and you want me to do this 'halal' (killing) with my own hands". And despite the fact that he would have to face so much criticism, he could not bring himself to refuse.

His practice of sending us to various parties to try and find some way out could sometimes result in highly embarrassing situations for us, especially as the Minister did not wish it disclosed that we had gone at his instance. One such experience I do not think I shall ever forget. When Shastriji took over as the Home Minister, Shri B.N. Jha was the Home Secretary. Although they had worked together in Uttar Pradesh, and also as Minister and Secretary in the Ministry of Communications, somehow in the Home Ministry they could not pull on well together. This was all the more strange, because Shastriji and Shri B.N. Jha resembled each other so much in character and their approach to life and work. Both were sober, ascetic, almost saintly persons, who lived for their work, and for whom work was worship. But Shastriji always had the uneasy feeling that Shri B.N. Jha, having had a giant like Pt. Govind Ballabh Pant as his Home Minister, was always in his mind comparing and contrasting him with his giant predecessor. Although like a good and disciplined civil servant Shri Jha would never say so, yet his manner seemed to indicate that things were far different and for the worse now. Also, Shri B.N. Jha, who was a firm believer in the principle that there could never be two swords in the same scabbard, did not take kindly to Shastriji taking the Additional Secretary, Shri L.P. Singh, as his adviser in some of his trouble-shooting missions. So all in all, when four months remained for Shri B.N. Jha's retirement, Shastriji was looking forward to his availing of leave before retirement. But Shri B.N. Jha showed no signs of obliging. So Shastriji suggested that I go and ask Shri Jha whether he would not like to avail of some leave. I reacted with horror and told him that when I was a probationer in the I.A.S., Shri B.N. Jha was the Chief Secretary of U.P., and we used to tremble at the very thought of entering his room. But still almost every day the Home Minister kept asking whether I had spoken to the Home Secretary, and once when I remonstrated, he exclaimed with some astonishment as to why in Service we are so nervous and fearful. This struck me as rather rich: here was the Home Minister of India who was hesitant to call his Home Secretary and ask him why he does not go on leave, and he was asking me, who had been a mere Probationer when the great man was Chief Secretary, to go and bell the cat. However, day in and day out the Minister kept asking, and I saw that there was going to be no escape. I was very much reminded of a beautiful Hindi poem of Shri Harivansh Rai Bachchan:

> *Jeevit bhi tu aaj mara sa*
> *Par meri to yah abhilasha*
> *Chita nikat bhi pahunch sakoon main*
> *Apne pairon pairon chalkar*
>
> (Even though alive you look as if you were dead. But it is my fervent wish that I may be able to walk on my own feet right up to my funeral pyre.)

I did not know whether Shri Harivansh Rai Bachchan would ever attain this cherished wish of being able to walk up to his own funeral pyre, but it seemed to me that I was coming precious near to doing so.

So one day plucking up all the courage I could muster and feeling very much like one who is going to attend his own funeral, I went and knocked on the great man's door. A deep voice said "Come in" and I pushed myself inside. The Home Secretary was working on some papers and he kept working on them, while I fidgeted about nervously and shifted from one leg to the other. There is nothing better calculated to demoralize a person as to make him feel that he is less important than even those scraps of papers. At this stage the great man looked up and with a curt nod beckoned me to be seated, while he kept on going through his files. So I sat and waited with my spirits sinking lower and lower, and my morale by that time had gone into the soles of my shoes.

Ultimately the Home Secretary looked up and asked in Hindi "How have you come?" Feigning an animation I could not feel, I babbled something that the Minister had been remarking several times that he (the Secretary) seemed to be undergoing great strain and tension, and though he (H.M.) would be sorry to lose his help, yet if the Secretary felt like taking leave, he would not stand in his way. There was a long and pregnant silence, after which the Home Secretary remarked." So the Minister has sent you"? I said "No Sir, No sir, it is just that he had been remarking about this so many times that I felt I should go and enquire". There was another deep silence, after which with a curl of the lip and a sneer he remarked. "*To aap yon hi shaukiya chale aye*" (So you have just come for the fun of it). It is difficult to convey the full shattering force of this remark in English, though a shudder still runs down my spine whenever I think of it.

There is a well-known saying that "No man is a hero to his valet." Perhaps equally it could be said that "No man is a hero to his SA" (Special Assistant). The relationship is too close, the points of contact too many to permit of hero worship. One cannot but be aware of the weaknesses as well as the strong points of the personality he serves. I do not think I am doing Lal Bahadurji an injustice when I say that he was most unsystematic and unmethodical in working, though he himself would have stoutly disagreed. About his hours of work and timings I shall come to later, but all the while one had the feeling that one just had to carry on oblivious of system and method, except that his aim and ambition was to clear every single file on his desk before leaving for home very late at night.

Particularly, there used to be great agony in drafting. Drafting is said to be a Civil Service disease, and every Civil Servant prides himself on his drafts. But whenever a carefully thought out and worked upon draft went to Shastriji he used his pencil on it with devastating effect. When a draft prided upon came back all mangled, maimed and mutilated, one's spirits sank to zero. However, much in the spirit of Rudyard Kipling's poem about watching "the things you gave your life to broken, and stoop and build them up with worn out tools", we would endeavour to repair the damage and re-submit, only to find it returning with further bleeding scars. Again and again drafts had to be typed and re-typed, and the effort was most exhausting for the personal staff.

Once, when he was Minister of Commerce and Industry there had been a significant improvement in export performance, and he wanted to bring this to the notice of the Prime Minister. I cannot keep count of how many times that letter was typed and re-typed, with no seeming end to the corrections he kept on making. The days passed into weeks, and the figures of statistics had to be continually revised to keep them up-to-date. Everyone breathed a sigh of relief when at long last the 'magnum opus' was issued.

Within 3 days the Prime Minister's reply was on his table. Shastriji was at that time on tour in Ernakulam in Kerala, and on seeing the envelope with the Prime Minister's Secretariat inscription, he opened it with some eagerness, only to feel completely dashed thereafter. The PM had written that he had taken note of the export performance, but that was all there was on the subject. The PM went on to say that he had heard incidentally that consumption of certain vegetable oils was harmful for human health, and hence we should endeavour to export more of them. When Shastriji was able to regain his spirits, he remarked on the strangeness of the suggestion that because certain vegetable oils were said to be harmful for health, we should ruin other people's health by exporting more of them. He went on to add ruefully that this is called quickness of disposal, for which the PM and people like Dr. Sampurnanand (then Chief Minister, U.P.) are famous. Whenever a paper alights upon your desk, you should immediately throw it up or throw it down, or to the right or to the left, or to anywhere, and this is hailed as speed of disposal; while those who wanted to give careful consideration and look into all the 'pros' and 'cons' before taking action, were condemned as indecisive and vacillating.

But the habit of continually revising drafts was one which never left him. At the Non-Aligned Summit in Cairo in October 1964, the text of the PM's speech was revised so many times that ultimately it could not be typed in full by the time he left for the Conference Hall. Part of the speech he took with him, while other parts were rushed to him in special vehicles with great difficulty through the tight security cordons as and when the typing could be done. For the last part we kept receiving frantic telephone calls from the Secretary to PM, Shri L.K. Jha, from the Conference Building. I recollect that when at last the concluding portion could be rushed to the Conference Building, Shri L.K. Jha was anxiously waiting outside the building, and he literally ran with it into the Conference Hall.

In fact, the manner in which Shastriji carried on at times was so exhausting, so taxing on his staff, that in moments of agony and exasperation the only way I could console myself was with the reflection that if only he had been working under me, instead of my working under him, I would have dismissed him from service.

CHAPTER 7

FIRMNESS WHEN SITUATION DEMANDED

I HAVE referred to his hesitation on several occasions in taking quick decisions, which gave the impression of indecisiveness. But in all fairness, one should also say that this appearance of indecisiveness was because of his deep-rooted love of compromise, and his desire to avoid hurting people. But when he felt that some step was necessary in the overall interest, or that some rank injustice was being done he did not hesitate in taking action.

One such instance was in the matter of the IAS pay scales in 1961-62. The case of the IAS was never referred to the Second Pay Commission, but an attempt was made to foist on this Service the scale recommended by the Pay Commission for the IFS (Indian Foreign Service) whose members were far less than the IAS, and whose conditions of service were totally different. Despite the protests of the IAS Associations, the matter was sought to be pushed through by the senior officers concerned of the ICS, and they even got the approval of the Cabinet for the same. But even at the 13th hour, when it was brought to Shastriji's notice in an informal note that a rank injustice was being done, he did not hestitate to re-open the whole issue. When the Senior Secretaries argued that a Cabinet decision had already been taken, he said that it was his responsibility to bring the matter before the Cabinet again, and he would not shirk his responsibility when he felt that something unfair was being done. It is entirely thanks to his sense of fair-play and resolute determination that justice was done to the IAS and it was given a much more equitable pay-scale.

There were various other matters where he held clear views, and refused to fall in line with proposals the senior officers wanted him to agree to without full consideration. One such matter was the pays to be drawn by ICS officers holding the posts of Special Secretary and Additional Secretary in the Government of India. While the pays existing at the time of Independence in 1947 were protected by Constitutional guarantee, there were no posts of Special Secretary and Additional Secretary at that time. The Comptroller and Auditor General (who belonged to a Service other than the ICS) had raised the point whether these posts, which did not exist at the time of the guarantee in the Constitution, were at all entitled to the special rates of pay of Rs.4000 and Rs.3500 per month respectively. This caused a flutter in the dovecotes of the ICS, and they sought to brush this objection aside. But Shastriji insisted that it was an important legal matter where the views of the Attorney General should be sought. A Statement of the Case was to be drawn up and sent to the Attorney General after the Home Minister's approval. But so perturbed were the senior officers of the ICS that the rather one-sided Statement of the Case drawn up by the Home Secretary and Finance Secretary was sent by them direct to the Attorney General, and only thereafter was the file put up to the Home Minister. Shastriji's note on the file at this stage was typical of him—a gentle rebuke but none the less clear and effective.

> "It seems that those concerned had not much faith in me, otherwise perhaps the Statement could have been shown to me before it was sent to the Attorney General. However, I have only to comment that this matter should be considered dispassionately. The ICS officers are no doubt concerned, but they need not make it a personal issue. It has a much wider implication. It would only be fair that Government gets an independent opinion and then finally makes up its mind."

In the matter of setting up the Central Bureau of Investigation (the now famous CBI), Shastriji as Home Minister, showed his determination. The proposal met with strong opposition from the Intelligence Bureau, whose very influential Director felt that the primacy of his position and that of his Organization was being eroded. All sorts of pressures were brought to bear, but once convinced of the need for a separate Bureau, Shastriji was resolute in taking the proposal through.

His capacity to take full responsibility stands out most clearly in the formation of the Cabinet after being chosen as the Prime Minister. Although he was chosen as the PM on a consensus basis, and the Congress President himself had spoken about collective leadership, Shastriji rightly felt that the formation of the Cabinet was not a matter for consensus, and it was the Prime Minister alone who had to take the responsibility. So, although some of his colleagues did not take kindly to it he did not consult anyone, not even the Congress President, Shri Kamaraj, in selecting his Council of Ministers. As he himself put it: "I can say without any fear of contradiction or without disrespect to any other colleagues that I have not consulted a single person in so far as the formation of my Cabinet was concerned. Even additions and alterations were made on my own."

The only two persons present in the room in 1, Moti Lal Nehru Place while he kept giving thought to this selection were his elder son-in-law, Shri Kaushal Kumar, and myself. We kept listening while the Prime Minister did his loud thinking and dictated names. To this day I have in my handwriting lists showing the posts in the Cabinet and in the full Council of Ministers, and the names of those he selected for the various posts, with pencilled amendments in his own hand when changes became necessary. And these changes had to be made throughout the day and even late into the night, depending on the reactions of some of those whom he had selected, when his choice was communicated to them.

One of the matters he was clear about was his eagerness to bring Indiraji into the Cabinet. After some initial reluctance about taking on new responsibilities so soon after her bereavement, she agreed and he offered her any portfolio of her choice. She herself selected Information and Broadcasting, and he gave her the No. 4 position in the Cabinet after Shri Gulzari Lal Nanda and Shri T.T. Krishnamachari.

Shastriji was also desirous of having Shri Morarji Desai in the Cabinet so that there would be no hard feelings after the latter had lost out in the 'consensus' for the PM's post. Likewise, he felt that others who had been "Kamarajed" with him in 1963 should get an opportunity to come back into the Government, and in this connection he thought of bringing back Shri Jagjiwan Ram. But during the discussions with Morarji Bhai, the latter made it clear that he could come back only if he was given the Number 2 position in the Cabinet. Shastriji felt that there was justification in his request, but he knew that this was something to which Shri G.L. Nanda and Shri T.T. Krishanamachari were implacably opposed, and even Shri Kamaraj and Indiraji would not favour it. So he tried to persuade Shri Morarji Desai to drop his insistence, but the latter pleaded that if he was to be brought into the Cabinet, he should be enabled to come with a feeling of self-respect. So reluctantly Shastri had to give up the idea of including Morarji Bhai, and thereafter, with much less reluctance, he decided to drop Shri Jagjiwan Ram as well, with whom also questions of seniority would be involved.

In the Planning Commission he was keenly desirous of having Shri R. Venkataraman, whose work as State Minister for Industries in Tamil Nadu had greatly impressed Shastriji during a visit to that State. He brought over Shri Venkataraman as a Member of the Planning commission in charge of Industries, and he always retained a great affection for and high expectations of him—expectations which time has shown have been more than justified by the present President of India.

Shastriji was also keen to cast his net wider than the political field, and bring in persons of eminence in their respective spheres. The two names he had in mind were Dr. Homi Bhabha and Dr. D.S. Kothari to be Ministers of State in independent charge of the Ministry of Atomic Energy and Scientific Development and the Ministry of Education respectively. This desire of his is of particular interest in the light of the induction last year of two top-ranking scientists in the National Front Government. But unlike these two scientists, both Dr. Bhabha and Dr. Kothari, when contacted, while thanking Shastriji profusely, begged him to excuse them, as they felt they could be more effective where they were than if they were enmeshed in the political arena. So much to his disappointment Shastriji had to give up this idea. And thus it was that the lists initially formulated by Shastriji kept getting chopped and changed, with the result that it was only late at night that he could go to the President with his final list.

At this point even at the cost of some diversion, one might

deal with the criticism of Shastriji for having given up Teen Murti House, which was the residence of the first PM, and was in every way suitable as an ear-marked residence for the Prime Minister, especially with the present-day elaborate security requirements. The result has been that every time a new Prime Minister takes office, a new residence has to be found and huge sums of money spent for making it suitable for a Prime Minister's requirements. It is a fact that the simple man that he was, Shastriji just could not reconcile himself to living in Teen Murti House, which had become closely identified over a long span of years with his giant predecessor. Moreover, he was very much attached to his residence, 1, Motilal Nehru Place, where his family still continues to reside. But some of us had brought him round to the idea of continuing to live at 1, Motilal Nehru Place, and treating Teen Murti House, or part of it, as the Official Residence of the Prime Minister, where his high level guests could be housed and official entertainments held. The example of Sri Lanka, where the then PM, Mrs. Sirimavo Bandaranaike resided at her Rosemead place residence, but "Temple Trees" was treated as the official residence of the Prime Minister seemed to attract him. But the gradual inclination on his part to this compromise arrangement was shattered by two events. The first was a letter from Indiraji in which she requested him to take an early decision about Teen Murti House—whether it would be made a memorial for her father or whether Shastriji intended moving into it. She went on to add that she had always felt that it was far too large a house for a residence, but her father's case was different because of the large crowds he used to attract. This would, however, not apply to any other. This letter rattled Shastriji, but still we hoped that he would come round to retaining Teen Murti House as the official residence of the PM. But even while he was reflecting on the matter, a few days later came a rather rudely worded letter from Smt. Krishna Huthee Singh, in that the present state of indecision about the Memorial was upsetting Indiraji, and that she was having occasional fainting fits. She virtually accused Shastriji of cruelty in delaying a decision about converting the House into a Memorial for Pt. Jawaharlal Nehru, as was being widely mooted. That letter sealed the fate of Teen Murti House. I still remember clearly Shastriji's pained re-action. In one of the few instances when he did not try to conceal his feelings, he tore the letter into little bits and flung it away, saying "I am not going anywhere near Teen Murti House".

To complete the story, later when Indiraji was the PM, a proposal was brought before the Cabinet for constructing a new official residence for the Prime Minister in the Rashtrapati Bhawan complex. At that time I was Joint Secretary to the Cabinet, where I had moved from the Prime Minister's Secretariat. Shri Morarji Desai, who was the Deputy Prime Minister as well as the Finance Minister, said he would never agree to such a huge expenditure, which was totally unjustified. He urged Indiraji to shift back into Teen Murti House, and pleaded that she was the only PM who could now do so. A separate Memorial could be set up for her father. Indiraji did not reject the proposal outright, though one of the younger Ministers expressed vehement opposition. There seemed a chance of the proposal being accepted, but by that time too many vested interests had been created, and eventually nothing came of it and the chance was lost for ever. And so it is that except when Shri Morarji Desai became PM and moved into 1, Safdarjang Road, everytime a new Prime Minister took over, a new residence had to be found for him and enormous expenditure incurred thereon. It is therefore, a welcome development that the former Prime Minister, Shri Vishwanath Pratap Singh, broke from this practice by moving into the Race Course Road residence of his predecessor. But the problem seems to be repeating itself with his successors.

CHAPTER 8

NO PITY ON HIMSELF—OR HIS STAFF

It is remarkable that he who had so much consideration for others had no pity on himself—or on his staff. The day was not his own—he used to be kept busy in meetings, Parliament, Party work etc., and he used to make it up by sitting in office till late at night. It was often around 11.00 p.m. or even midnight that he left for home, and while on tour I can recollect one or two instances when work went on all through the night. Sometimes he would remark that he had spoilt his habits, and would urge us not to spoil our habits with him. On Sundays and holidays I would avoid going on my own, but often-times, the call would come. Then he used to remark somewhat apologetically that Sunday was the only day for my family, and that I should not waste the whole day here, but should definitely go home by lunch time. Having said which, he used to give me enough work to keep me occupied till Doomsday.

He also had a fancy for drawing up timetables, and many a time these timetables were duly drawn up, in which the various timings throughout the day were meticulously given. On some of them he used to add a sentence in his own handwriting—"S A will leave the Office at 8.30 p.m. sharp". I used to gaze ruefully at this order when sitting in office beyond 10.00 or 11.00 p.m. night after weary night.

When Shri L.K. Jha took over in mid-1964 as Secretary to the Prime Minister, he remarked that this was an impossible way of working and that we should have a proper timetable and adhere to it. I told him that I had been working with Shastriji for 5½ years up to that time, and it was impossible to get him to work to any timetable. However, Shri L.K. Jha broached the subject with the PM and he came back and said that the PM was highly enthusiastic and altogether in favour. He went on to remark that perhaps we had not been able to put up the matter in the correct perspective. So Mr. L.K. Jha went on to draw up his timetable and get the PM's approval, after which copies were sent to all of us for strict adherence. But within three days Shri L.K. Jha was tearing his hair and saying that so many people are ringing me up, and I just do not know where the PM is. He asked me whether I knew. I could not resist the temptation of getting a bit of my own back by looking at his freshly circulated timetable, and saying that according to your timetable he should be here itself.

How great was the gap between good intention and implementation can best be brought out by what happened on the night of Shri Feroze Gandhi's cremation in September 1960. Shastriji had come straight back from the Nigambodh burning ground to Udyog Bhawan, and he was talking about the scenes at the burning ghat. He mentioned that Panditji (Jawaharlalji) in particular was deeply distressed, and that he kept saying that every one had been advising Feroze to exercise some caution, but he would not listen, and this was the ultimate result. All at once the PM remarked "Lal Bahadur, you are also a heart patient (Shastriji had a heart attack in October 1959 while in Allahabad). I hear you keep sitting in office till very late at night. This is a very wrong thing to do. You should take proper care and make it a point to leave office by 8 p.m.

Shastriji said that it would be difficult to leave by 8 p.m. but since Jawaharlalji had been so affectionate and considerate, he had decided that he would now not sit in office beyond 9.00 p.m. On hearing this, I and the other members of the Personal Staff felt like jumping with joy, because the prospect of being able to get back home by 9.00 p.m. was a good fortune we could hardly have dreamt of. Shastriji was in a very emotional and reminiscent mood, and he kept speaking of his early life and his association with the Nehru family, and of the up-and-down relationship between Indira and Feroze. While he was still speaking, the clock suddenly struck nine. He stopped with a guilty start and said, "The whole evening has gone and we have not done a stroke of work". I told him he need not worry, I would come to his residence early next morning, and in a couple of hours all the files would be disposed of. At this, he got up and said that at least on the first night we should adhere to the schedule decided upon. But he kept looking guiltily at the pile of files, and then asked whether there were not some files that just required signatures. I told him there were a few such files, but they could easily wait till morning. On this he remarked that leaving a pile of files unattended was like carrying their load on his mind, and he would like to lighten it to some extent. So we started on the signature files, and then we went on to other files, and then still more files, until the whole heap had been gone through. And with Panditji's advice to Shastriji ringing in our ears, it was close upon midnight when we crawled wearily home.

It was these long and lonely night hours that made working with him something of a torture. There was no family life, no social life, no games, no sports, no music, no outings, in fact no sort of life at all, apart from work, work and more work. By the time, I returned home close upon midnight, everybody would be fast asleep, and only the Alsatian dog kept jumping and jumping with joy to greet me on return. Rather than eating a cold dinner late at night, for a few days I started coming back for a quick dinner and then returning to office. But instead of resting and relaxing after the night meal, the prospect of rushing back to office proved so hateful that I soon gave it up. At times I thought of following his injunction and returning home by 8.30 p.m. But I realized that in that case I would not be of much use to him—indeed, I might as well not be there at all. It was only during those late night hours that he did his serious work, and it was at that time that he unburdened himself and took us into confidence on the passing events of the day and his own reactions to them. It was only then that we could get glimpses of his inmost thoughts.

But even the importance of the matters that were being handled did not take away from the strain of such an existence. After two or three years of this life, I developed asthma and began to pass sleepless nights. The doctors urged that I should get away and have a period of rest. But when I mentioned this to Shastriji, he remarked that this is exactly what is wrong with doctors. They understand neither the ailment nor the remedy, and hence they fall back on rest, as if rest is everything in the world. "*Yahi to doctoron mein kharabi hai. Na unke marz samajh mein aati hai na dawa, bas ek aaram ka sahara le lete hain, jaise aaram hi duniya mein sab kuch hai.*" And his parting injuction to me was not to bother about taking leave but to work less—which, I think he knew as well as I, was a virtual impossibility.

It was a situation from which there was no escape. In my despair I went to the Cabinet Secretary, only to be told that since I was attached to an important Minister there was nothing he could do to help in getting me relieved. His parting remark in jocular vein only added to my gloom: "If you want to get away, stop working, and he will himself throw you out."

There was another factor also that made working with Shastriji something of a handicap. With his strict notions of propriety, he was not prepared to do anything for those connected with him lest he be accused of mis-using his influence and bestowing favours; leave alone going out of his way to help, this used to be the case even when something worth-while would have come their way in the normal course. This used to result in deeply mortifying situations. On the one hand, one was told that his work with the Minister was so important that he could not be relieved, while on the other, all the promotion opportunities and fellowships for going abroad etc. went to those presumably doing less important work. It was always a case of 'Heads, I lose, Tails, you win.' Seeing how some others benefitted from their connections with Ministers or important Secretaries, one could not help reflecting bitterly that one stood to lose so much by being associated with Shastriji.

In the relationship between Special Assistant/Private Secretary and Minister, there are some who came into the limelight while holding the post of SA/PS. Maybe they could carry it off, and of course much depended on the personality and political weight of the Minister to whom they were attached. In any case, with so modest and unassuming a Minister as Shastriji, it would have been incongruous for the SA to go throwing his weight around. Nor is it necessary. My own experience is that the more the SA/PS keeps himself in the background, the more effective and influential he becomes. Parading his own importance or taking credit for decisions is a dis-service to the Minister. It is the gentle hint, the modest suggestion, in complete privacy, that carries the most weight and helps at times to influence policy.

This was very much my experience. How completely I kept in

the background can be gauged by the fact that despite seven years of working so closely and intimately with him, I hardly appear in any of his innumerable photographs.

I had mentioned earlier his habit of phrasing his instructions in question form: "*Aap saath chalna pasand karenge*?", (Would you like to come along?) Despite the softness and the gentleness of the phrasing, it was, as I have remarked, like a commandment written on stone, as will be exemplified from the following instance. In January 1964, Pt. Jawaharlal Nehru had fallen seriously ill at Bhubaneshwar, and Shastriji, who had resigned under the Kamaraj Plan, was brought back into the Cabinet as Minister without Portfolio to assist the Prime Minister. It was just my luck that his return to the Cabinet more or less coincided with my return to India after the six months' "escape" on a Nuffield Foundation Fellowship. Shastriji straightway sent for me and suggested that I rejoin him. I pleaded that I had already worked four and a half years with him, and on my going away to the U.K. he had taken on my younger brother, who had spent only a few months with him before his resignation and could be called back again. Moreover, I was under orders of reversion to U.P. and was expecting my posting any day. Shastriji just remarked, "Let us think over it for a few days".

Just a few days later, I was lying in bed running a temperature. I remember clearly that it was the 29th January, the evening of the Beating of the Retreat Ceremony. Also that it was a bitterly cold winter. Sometime after the Retreat was over, Shastriji's telephone call came. He said that the loss and subsequent recovery of the Sacred Relic of Hazratbal in Kashmir had created all sorts of tensions, that passions were running high and that it looked as if the Valley was going up in flames. The ailing Prime Minister had asked Shastriji to go at once to Kashmir and had authorized him to deal with the sitaution on the spot. Shastriji said that he was flying to Srinagar early the next morning, and then came the favourite (and dreaded) phrase; "*Aap saath chalna pasand karenge*?" I replied that I would like to very much, but I was going back to U.P. in the next few days and had already received my posting orders as Director of Industries. How could I now go to Kashmir? To this, Shastriji responded that the visit to Kashmir was just for a few days to sort out a

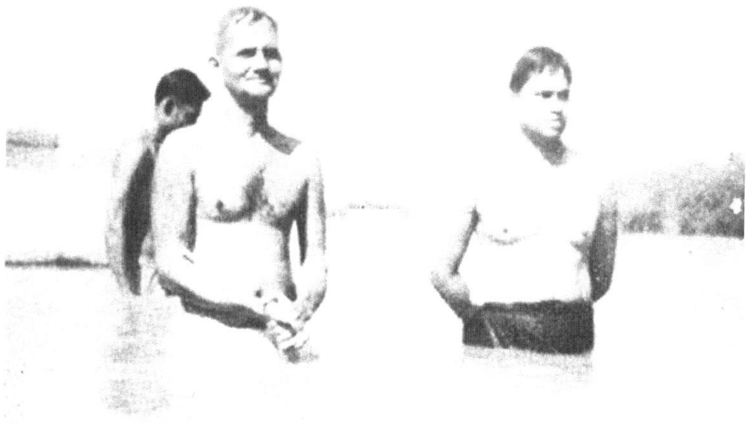

Author with Shri Lal Bahadur Shastri taking bath in the river Ganges at Rishikesh (June 1960)

Shri Lal Bahadur Shastri as Home Minister along with other officers at the farewell function to the author (April 1963)

Prime Minister Lal Bahadur Shastri, photographed with the President of Yugoslavia, Marshal Tito, during the last Summit Conference of Non-aligned Nations in Cairo in October 1964

Prime Minister Lal Bahadur Shastri, greeting the Rt. Hon'ble Earl Mountbatten of Burma at the lunch given by the President in honour of the visiting dignitary in New Delhi on May 5, 1965

Prime Minister Lal Bahadur Shastri was given a rousing reception at Allahabad airport on Aprin 16, 1965. In the photograph the Prime Minister is seen garlanding a child in return

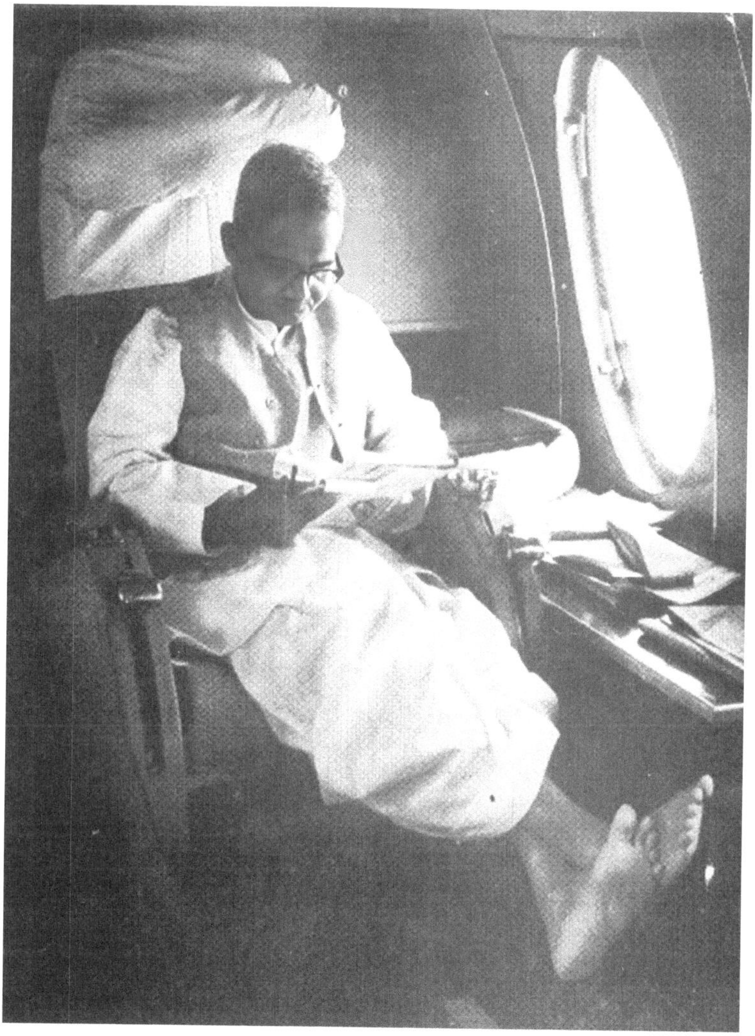

Lal Bahadur Shastri studying papers during a flight

Lal Bahadur Shastri at work

Lal Bahadur Shastri with his wife Lalita Shastri

The last photograph, Tashkent, 10th January, 1966

critical situation, and on return these matters could be looked into. When this excuse of mine proved to be of no avail, then I brought out what I thought would be the ultimate weapon. I told him that I was lying ill in bed and running a temperature, and that the doctors had advised that I should guard against exposure to the severe cold. Prompt came the response: "*Han, so to voh bilkul theek kahate hain, aap khoob kambal vambal orh kar aaiyega* (Yes, they are perfectly right. You should come carefully wrapped up in blankets.) And thus it was, that on the morning of the 30th January 1964, I found myself duly wrapped up in my blankets shivering in several feet of snow in Srinagar. And "the few days" were to end only with his departure from this earthly existence.

An example of the difference between what he said out of courtesy, and what he really felt, was in connection with vegetarianism. Shastriji was a staunch vegetarian and proud of it. How fervently he believed in it can be illustrated in one instance when at the request of the then Deputy Minister, Food & Agriculture, Shri Krishnappa, he had agreed to inaugurate an All India Cattle Show in Karnataka. However, when the papers concerning the Show were received. Shastriji was taken aback to find that it was an "All India Cattle and Poultry Show". He immediately rang up Shri Krishnappa and requested the latter to excuse him, because he (Shri Krishnappa) had brought poultry into it, and he (Shastriji) would not like to get mixed up with poultry. However, Shri Krishnappa pleaded with him not tc change his programme at that late stage, as all the cards etc. had been printed and issued. Very reluctantly Shastriji agreed.

Knowing Shastriji's sentiments. I just mentioned poultry once each in the opening and closing sentences of his draft Address. But Shastriji firmly struck out even these references to poultry and said that he was going to inaugurate a Cattle Show, and would take no notice of poultry.

At the Conference itself, the assembled Directors of Animal Husbandry and others spoke of the superior breeds of cattle they were developing and the increased yields of milk etc. They also proudly spoke of the improved strains of poultry, how these improved birds laid so many more eggs and were delicious *table birds* and so on. Poor Shastriji sat impassive, but squirming inwardly at these recitals. When it came to his turn to inaugurate the Show, he read out his speech just as it was, without any reference to poultry.

However, when he finished, he felt it looked odd not to have said a word about poultry, about which so many speakers had waxed eloquent throughout the afternoon. So rather haltingly he said; "You have said something about poultry also, but I do not know anything about it, because I am a vegetarian. So I will leave it to my friend Krishnappa to increase its production as well as its consumption", and sat down.

In the light of these strong feelings of his, it seemed odd that often when we travelled by air, and the Air Hostess asked "Vegetarian or Non-Vegetarian", I would say, "Two Vegetarian", upon which Shastriji would immediately interrupt to say "One Non-Vegetarian." I would insist on "Two Vegetarian", and he would repeat "One Non-Vegetarian", until the poor Air Hostess would look completely bewildered. Then I would tell her firmly, "Please don't listen to him, kindly bring only two vegetarian". Shastriji out of his innate courtesy would then say that since you take non-vegetarian food, why should you deny yourself just for my sake. On which I would point out that we were virtually vegetarians at home, that my mother and my wife were staunch vegetarians, and it was only because of my upbringing and education abroad, and living in boarding houses and hostels that I had taken to non-vegetarian food. In any case, I just would not take non-vegetarian food in his presence.

So time and again we used to go through this pantomime, but the grim reality was something quite different. Shastriji was flying back from Manipur and at the halt at Agartala the Chief Commissioner, Tripura, who hailed from Orissa, had said that he would arrange for lunch at the aerodrome itself (it could hardly be called an airport in those days). There was a small room and a small table. Before, Shastriji and his P.A. Shri Venkataraman, vegetarian food was served. But before Shri Kuldip Nayar (then the Home Minister's Press Officer) and myself, two plates were placed with pieces of chicken with the bones sticking up. I immediately asked for it to be taken away, but the Chief Commissioner's wife, who was the hostess, said that she was told that some in the party were non-vegetarians and she had specially prepared this dish and now no one was prepared to touch it. Seeing how hurt the hostess was feeling. Kuldip Nayar and I looked at each other and took up our knife and fork and started eating. Just then a dish of fish was also brought. But feeling that sufficient unto the day is the evil thereof, I straightaway requested for it to be taken away. All this time Shastriji had said not a word, but now he spoke up: "*Arre jab aap voh garhbarh wali cheez kha rahe hain to isme kyon hichak rahe hain?*" (When you are eating that unwholesome thing then why are you jibbing at this?) He then went on to expound that if a meat dish does not look like meat he can still tolerate it; but when all these bones are sticking out, then it becomes very hurtful. One can just imagine the plight of Kuldip and myself. We did not know what to do with the morsel in our mouths—whether to throw it out, or with a supreme effort try to force it down, or whether like Lord Shiva, to keep it in our throats and forever after be known like him as 'Neelkanth' (Blue-throated).

For the whole afternoon, Shastriji was in anything but a good mood. At night in Calcutta, Shri Tushar Kanti Ghosh of the Amrit Bazar Patrika' had arranged for a dinner at his residence. Some programme delayed Shastriji and he had to exuse himself from going for the dinner. But with his habitual courtesy, he insisted that the members of his staff and other accompanying officers should go. At the residence of Shri Tushar Kanti Ghosh, there was a lavish spread, both vegetarian and non-vegetarian. But with the experience of the afternoon in mind, I strictly avoided the non-vegetarian dishes. On our return to Dum Dum Airport at night. Shastriji with the consideration usual to him, inquired whether we had had our dinner. But to me he asked whether there was non-vegetarian food also. I told him that there was both vegetarian and non-vegetarian, to which in front of everybody he said: "*Chalo, achcha hua, aapko phir vahi chicken vikan khane ko mil gaya hoga*" (That's good, you must have got the chance of eating chicken once again). After all the pantomime in the plane journeys, at this one departure from my strict practice of never taking non-vegetarian food in his presence, he was utterly unsparing.

Another humorous sidelight on his love of vegetarianism concerns his First PA, Shri V.S. Venkataraman, presently Additional Secretary in the Commerce Ministry. Outwardly Shri Venkataraman was a pure vegetarian, but off the beaten track he liked eating eggs. Shastriji's ways were so informal that sometimes they led to piquant situations. Many a time on tour, while staying in Raj Bhawans, there used to be a gentle knock on the door, and the Prime Minister would walk in. Sometimes one would be found standing on his neck (*Sarvangasana*) and sometimes standing on his head (*Sheershasana*), or in some awkward pose. Once when there was a gentle knock on Shri Venkataraman's door and the Prime Minister entered, Shri Venkataraman was busy eating an egg and got caught red-handed. For sometime after, this egg continued to haunt Shri Venkataraman, like the dead albatross which was hung round the neck of the Ancient Mariner in Coleridge's famous poem. When visiting a place, Shastriji always made it a point to introduce his staff, and for sometime Shri Venkataraman's introduction used to be something like this: "He is Shri Venkataraman, a very young and smart First PA. As his name indicates, he is a South Indian Brahmin, and the South Indian Brahmins have the proudest tradition of vegetarianism in the whole of India. Here is the inheritor of a proud tradition, who has reduced himself to hiding in his room and eating eggs."

CHAPTER 9

"PRISONERS OF INDECISION"

IN A previous Chapter (7), I have referred to instances where Shastriji showed he could be resolute and acted firmly. But these and other instances of decisiveness on his part were not known to the general public or to the world at large. To them he appeared to be a meek and mild person, who in his search for compromise solutions was unable to make up his mind, and was incapable of swift and decisive action. It required a crisis of the dimensions of war and national peril to reveal that he could also be a man of action. There was steel beneath the velvet, no matter how deeply concealed. And he displayed this quality to the nation and the world in what proved to be his shining hour in the last year of his earthly existence—during the 1965 War with Pakistan.

The early part of 1965 was a particularly bad period for the Shastri Government. Economic conditions in the country had worsened, and prices kept soaring. Language riots had inflicted deep wounds, and fissiparous tendencies had started raising their head. In international relations the trouble in the Rann of Kutch had caused deep concern, and its aftermath, the Kutch Agreement, had not aroused any enthusiasm; in fact, the Prime Minister was hard put to defend it. Everywhere the general impression was gaining ground that the Prime Minister was weak and irresolute, and unable to give the lead which the country so sorely needed. In Parliament Smt. Vijayalakshmi Pandit put it forcefully when she said that "The Prime Minister and his colleagues have become prisoners of indecision." The Press took up the cry, and for sometime, everywhere, on all sides, one kept hearing the phrase "Prisoners of indecision".

It was but natural that the leaders of Pakistan also shared the widely-prevailing impression. In fact, Mr. Z.A. Bhutto, the

Foreign Minister, had gone so far as to say that "The leadership of India is in disarray". It must have occurred to them that if ever there was a time to strike, it was now. First it was in the nature of a probe in the Kutch area, and then when that appeared to be succeeding, in the form of a full-scale offensive to obtain their most cherished objective of winning back Kashmir.

At first these calculations appeared to be correct. While there was a general outcry in the country against the Pakistan aggression in Kutch, the Prime Minister's reaction was much more restrained. To the general demand for strong action, his feeling was that while aggression could not be tolerated, yet some restraint should be exercised, lest hostilities aggravate into a full-scale war with Pakistan.

He was in Kathmandu, Nepal, after the inauguration of the Kosi Barrage towards the end of April 1965, when the first report came in of Pakistan having used armour in Kutch. There was a banquet at the Indian Embassy where the King and Queen of Nepal were present. A recitation of King Mahendra's poems was going on, and the PM was nodding and clapping to show his appreciation. At about 11 p.m. there was a trunk call from Delhi, and my counterpart, the other Joint Secretary in the PM's Secretariat, conveyed the grave news. I went and quietly whispered this in the PM's ears. Not by the flicker of an eyelid did he show any signs of emotion or agitation, and he kept on nodding and saying "*Khoob*" and "*Bahut Sundar*" (Excellent and very beautiful), as the poems were being recited.

But an hour later, when he was back in the Royal Guest House at Sheetal Niwas, he kept pacing the floor, and said that we had asked General Chaudhuri (then Chief of the Army Staff) to consider sending tanks into the Rann of Kutch area, and he had replied, "That desert. . . . I would not waste even an old tin can there." And now, Shastriji went on to say, Pakistan had done precisely that. Like other top-rank Government Officers, General Chaudhuri could take shelter behind the political leadership, but he as Prime Minister would have to face the full blast of the people's anger.

And face the full blast of the people's anger he did. There was a general outcry for India taking strong counter-measures. and also for sending its own armour into the Kutch area. But Shastriji continued to resist the cry for all-out action. He reiterated his life-long devotion to peace and non-violence, and said that as a follower of Gandhi and Nehru, he could be no party to a war with Pakistan. War with Pakistan would mean the ruin of both countries, and he would first try and take every step to avoid such a calamity. Although it required great courage he held fast, and after the Commonwealth Prime Minister's Conference in London in June 1965, he entered into long-drawn negotiations with President Ayub Khan through the good offices of the British Premier, Mr. Harold Wilson. There were days and nights of negotiation, but ultimately with the help of Mr. Wilson, the Kutch Agreement was hammered out, whereby it was agreed to refer the disputed points to arbitration. Mr. Wilson wanted to announce the Agreement then and there in London itself, but Shastriji was too shrewd a politician to take any hasty step. He wanted to involve his colleagues in the Government also, and therefore insisted that the Agreement would be announced only after he and President Ayub had returned to their respective countries and consulted their colleagues.

His apprehensions proved correct. When the Kutch Agreement was placed before the Cabinet, it met with considerable criticism, but he took it through. The reaction in the Congress Working Committee was even less enthusiastic, but he prevailed. And when the All India Congress Committee met in the Lal Bagh in Bangalore, after his detailed justification of the Agreement, all that he could get was that the AICC took note of the PM's Statement on the Kutch Agreement. But despite all the opposition and criticism, he stood fast, and kept re-iterating his own life-long and the country's devotion to peace, and abhorrence of the prospect of war with Pakistan.

It was this display of courage that the rulers of Pakistan mistook for weakness. Having succeeded somewhat in their Kutch adventure, they must have reasoned that now was the time and the opportunity to strike, and launch the far bigger adventure of overrunning Kashmir. They could not have made a greater mistake, or misjudged their man more completely. The boy who punished himself by jumping into the Ganga because he had mis-spent the fare for the ferry, the freedom fighter who *was not prepared* to seek parole to go to the bedside of his dying daughter, the Railway Minister who insisted on accepting responsibility and resigning over a Railway disaster for which he was in no way to blame—all these showed the mettle of the man, and indicated the steel beneath the velvet. But of these the Rulers of Pakistan were not aware, or perhaps did not take them into account, and launched what became for them a terrible mis-adventure, and ended up with the Indian Army sitting on the outskirts of Lahore and Sialkot.

I still remember vividly the 5th of August 1965 when the change came about in Shastriji's attitude. It was a day of some religious festival, and Smt. Shastri had performed puja, and thereafter we all sat down for dinner on the floor eating from "Pattals" (leaves used as plates). On such occasions the members of the Personal Staff joined the family and were treated just like them. Although Shastriji himself had not much faith in religious ceremonial, and believed firmly that work was the best form of worship, yet he fully respected his wife's beliefs, and stood by her side at all these ceremonies. It was while we were sitting on the floor and eating that he quietly remarked that he had learnt that while he was negotiating in all sincerity with President Ayub in London, the Razakars (Pak infiltrators) were being trained in Murree. He was now convinced of President Ayub's malafides, and it seemed that war had now become inevitable. Sad though he was at the prospect, he was resolved to see it firmly through. Once again he acted on his mother's advice given to him long years back when he first gave up his studies to join the Freedom Struggle to the consternation and anger of his relatives: "Think well before you act, but once having decided, never look back".

CHAPTER 10

WAR WITH PAKISTAN: HIS SHINING HOUR

AND THUS with the hour came the man. Despite his life-long devotion to peace, when the trumpets of war sounded, he became the resolute man of action who led his nation fearlessly into the struggle. Speaking from the ramparts of the Red Fort on Independence Day, the 15th of August 1965, he made his stirring call to the nation: "*Hum hathiyar ka jawab hathiyar se denge*" (Force will be met by force) and "*Hum rahen ya na rahen, ye desh bana rahe, ye jhanda laharata rahe,*" (Whether we remain or not let this country remain strong, and let this flag keep flying).

And so it was that when the Army Chiefs asked for permission to cross the Cease Fire Line in Kashmir it was readily given. Then on the 1st of September came the devastating full-scale onslaught by Pakistan in the Chhamb-Jaurian Sector of Jammu with tanks and heavy artillery. The Armed Forces asked for the Indian Air Force to be thrown in. The Prime Minister only remarked that it would represent a major escalation of the fighting, and that we had avoided it in the Chinese War of 1962. But on being told that it was essential in order to halt the Pakistani attack and save our troops from slaughter, he agreed, and the Air Force was brought into the fray.

Yet on the next day the Army Chief again approached him and mentioned the desperate situation in the Chhamb Sector because of the heavy weight of tanks and artillery thrown in by Pakistan. Shastriji asked why do you not send more tanks there, to which the reply was that the bridge over the river Chenab at Akhnoor could not take the weight of heavy armour. On the other hand, Pakistan could readily deploy its tanks over the plains of West Pakistan bordering Jammu. Somewhat distressed, the PM asked "Is there no way out?" To which the Army Chief replied, "There is only one way out, and that is if we go into Pakistan ourselves". Shastriji hesitated just a moment—after all, the decision was a very grave one, and then quietlv said, "Then do it"

It was a decision of tremendous consequence to attack Pakistan in its very heartland. The courage in taking such a decision has to be assessed in the background of the military debacle of 1962, when the morale of the Armed Forces slumped to its lowest. India's prestige as a military power was in mud at that time, and this, added to what they considered to be a leadership in disarray, had emboldened the leaders of Pakistan in their aggressive venture. It was therefore, no ordinary decision to invade Pakistan in the Punjab, where its armed forces were at their strongest.

So grave was the decision that the Army Chief wanted to leave no doubt about the imponderability of the consequences "Sir, I take it you know what this is going to mean," he is reported to have said. To which the Prime Minister quietly replied." I know what it is going to mean, and that is why I am asking you to do it".

The Army Chief asked for sometime to contact his Commanders in the field. He spoke personally to all of them, and came back the next day to report to the P.M. "Sir you are right. Our boys are full of beans and spoiling for a fight. We will go into Pakistan".

Having taken this momentous decision, the PM gave the Armed Forces their head and left detailed decisions on tactics and strategy to them. Although the small Emergency Committee of the Cabinet (ECC) was meeting daily, and sometimes more than once a day, it did not get bogged down in details, and concentrated on matters of overall policy and direction, and mobilizing support for the Armed Forces. Shastriji had seen what had happened during the Chinese invasion of 1962, and was determined that those mistakes would not be repeated.

In 1962 he had been the Home Minister, and the North East Sector was under his special charge. He had visited Assam in late October and had gone to Tezpur. It was Diwali night, but there was the darkness of the black-out evervwhere, and even the public meetings had to be held in the headlights of surrounding jeeps. Speaker after speaker vowed to fight the advancing enemy to the last, and shed his blood if need be. Shastriji also visited the Corps Headquarters and met Lt. General Harbaksh Singh, who had taken over command, as General B.M. Kaul had taken ill and gone back to Delhi. It was late at night, and with the aid of the huge maps on the wall Gen. Harbaksh Singh gave the Home Minister a full briefing. At the end of it, Shastriji asked, "General, are you hopeful of holding the enemy? "to which the General replied. "Hopeful? I am confident."

Greatly re-assured, Shastriji left Assam, but on reaching Calcutta he learnt to his dismay that Gen. Kaul was being sent back to Tezpur as the Corps Commander. He rushed back to Delhi and pleaded with the P.M. that he had just come from Tezpur, that Gen Harbaksh Singh was in full control and that a change at this juncture might upset everything. But Pt. Nehru refused to hear anything against Gen. Kaul and said that he is our finest soldier; he had been taken unwell and had to come away, but he is fully recovered now and wants another chance to prove himself, and I have so decided.

So Gen. Kaul went back to Tezpur and to the Command of the Corps, with consequences that are known to all. The Chinese advance through NEFA was so swift that it seemed that any day they would debouch into the plains of Assam and overrun North Assam. The Assam Government got the feeling that the Army was intending to withdraw from Assam and represented strongly against any such move. The Emergency Committee of the Union Cabinet issued firm orders that the Army would not leave Assam, but would fall back to the South Bank of the river Brahmaputra. The Governor, Shri Vishnu Sahay, was authorized to decide whether and when the rail and road bridge over the Brahmaputra should be blown up, a bridge that had only recently been completed with so much cost and labour. But Pt. Jawaharlal's broadcast about our hearts going out to our countrymen in Assam in their hour of trial, though deeply felt and sincerely meant, was misunderstood in Assam to mean that they were being left alone, and there was the Chief Minister, Shri B.P. Chaliha's despairing statement that in the *hour of our* agony we are being abandoned by our countrymen.

In these trying circumstances, the Home Minister was asked

to proceed at once to Assam and re-assure the Government and people of Assam that the rest of India would stand by them to the end. He was also to assist the State Government in maintaining the essential services and the administration, which were reported to be breaking down in the areas North of the Brahmaputra. Before day-light on the 21st October Shastriji set out for Palam Airport to take the special plane to Tezpur. At that time the Chinese were advancing so fast that we half expected them to be in the vicinity of Tezpur by the time we reached. However, just as Shastriji reached Palam Airport he got the amazing and totally unexpected news of the unilateral Cease Fire declared by the Chinese. He rushed back to Teen Murti House to inquire what should now be done, but it was decided that he should go through with the programme in any case.

Tezpur was in shambles by the time he reached. Gen Kaul was there looking pale and shaken. The previous Deputy Commissioner had deserted his charge and fled, the Treasury had been emptied, currency notes had been burnt and there was no administration worth the name. The one thing visible was the relief writ large on the faces of the Chief Minister and everybody else at the unexpected Unilateral Cease Fire which was being regarded as a God-send when everything had seemed lost. Shastriji flew from place to place on that sad and sorrowful day with Shri Biju Patnaik, and the impressions of chaos and confusion he gathered never left his mind.

Now that he was himself the Prime Minister, he was clear in his mind that the mistakes of 1962 should not be repeated, and there should be no unnecessary meddling in the details of operations etc. While giving full support and encouragement to the Generals and Air Marshals, he avoided breathing down their necks all the time. On the other hand, he concentrated on mobilizing the tremendous enthusiasm of the people and chanelling it in directions required for the war effort. The slogan he gave of "Jai Jawan, Jai Kisan" electrified the nation, and the whole country rose as one behind their newly discovered supreme leader.

By the spirit and qualities he displayed at this time of supreme crisis, Shastriji proved worthy of their confidence. Never more so, than when the Chinese issued their 3-day ultimatum requiring India to remove "defence structures" which they alleged had been put up in their territory near the Border with Sikkim. This was obviously a pretext to try and intervene in aid of their ally Pakistan. Shastriji pointed out the ridiculousness of the ultimatum which, even if their charges were correct (which they were absolutely not), would have required Indian troops re-entering Chinese territory to remove these so-called structures. At such a time, when in addition to the hostilities with Pakistan, the prospect of war with China loomed large, Shastriji remained calm and composed and refused to be brow-beaten. His statements in Parliament on the Chinese threat are those of a great leader who knew his mind and was determined not to be cowed down by threats or be over-awed by the overwhelming gravity of the situation. The courage and resolution shown by him must have been one of the factors that compelled the Chinese to decide against this adventurism, apart from the clearly indicated opposition of both the Superpowers, U.S.A. and U.S.S.R, to any Chinese involvement.

It was in this connection that he made one of his infrequent interventions in strategy decisions. On being informed by the Defence Minister, Shri Y.B. Chavan, that the Chief of Air Staff, Air Chief Marshal Arjan Singh, wanted to bomb East Pakistan, he asked the Defence Minister not to allow it and to dissuade the Air Chief. The Defence Minister again contacted him and said that the Chief of Air Staff felt aggrieved by the decision and wanted to represent personally to the Prime Minister about it.

The Air Chief Marshal came all tense and taut, determined to fight out the issue with the PM. But instead of receiving him in the main office Room at 10, Janpath, with all the war maps and charts etc, Shastriji led him to the adjacent small ante-room, where the table was laid out for tea with sweets and samosas etc. For quite sometime the PM continued to converse on almost any topic except the War, which must have greatly puzzled the Air Chief, as well as helped to cool him down. At last after the tea was over, the Prime Minister gently said that the Defence Minister had informed him that you wanted permission to bomb East Pakistan. At this the Air Chief became tense again and said: "Look at those cowardly attacks on Kalaikunda and Bagdogra (Airfields). My men have been killed and my planes destroyed. You just give the word and I shall go and bomb the hell out of East Pakistan". The PM calmly replied: "*Air Chief Marshal Sahib, Aap to sipahi hain, aur siphai ka khoon to garam hota hai. Par mujh jaisa chhota admi, agar mera khoon garam hota, to na jane main zindagi mein kitni bar pit gaya hota*". (Air Chief Marshal Sahib, you are a warrior, and a warrior's blood is always hot. But if a small man like me had been hot-blooded, I do not know how many times I would have been beaten up.) "So I have learned to be very cautious, and to think well before deciding on any step. Now I have been informed that any action by us in East Pakistan is the pretext that China is waiting for to intervene in the fighting, and this has been confirmed by the Intelligence of the USA and the USSR. So I do not want to give China an excuse to get involved. If despite all our forbearance, China still decides to come in, then, to use your own words, go and bomb the hell out of East Pakistan. Until then, kindly hold your hand." To which the Air Chief promptly replied. "Yes Sir, I understand. Your orders will be complied with"

In his quiet, calm and resolute manner he led his nation to victory in the war which had been forced upon him. Pakistan must have rued the day when it embarked upon its misadventure, because at the time of the Cease Fire brought about by the United Nations, the Indian Army was sitting on the outskirts of Lahore and Sialkot, and in Pak-occupied Kashmir, highly strategic points like the Haji-Pir Pass had been over-run by the Indian forces. The morale of the Indian Armed Forces which had plumbed the depths in 1962, soared to new peaks in 1965. When Lt. General Harbaksh Singh, G.O.C. in C of the Western Command (under which the operations were conducted) was asked to what he attributed the success of Indian arms in this war, he said it was due to the valour, heroism and self-sacrifice of our younger officers and men, who literally threw themselves to their deaths, and to that brave little man who is our Prime Minister. Never was a truer word spoken.

The reaction of his aged mother when given the news was simpler: "*Nanku jeet gaya*" (Nanku—his pet name—has won). And Shastriji put it in his own inimitable manner with his quiet humour. After the Cease Fire he flew to the Northern Air bases, and from there by helicopter he went to several places in Pakistan under Indian Army occupation, and addressed the soldiers in the field. At one such place he said: "*Yeh Pakistani sochte hain ki Hindu to larh hi nahin sakta. Halanki hum bar bar kahte hain ki Hindustan to aur bhi kaumon ka watan hai, voh to samajhte hain ki Hindustan to Hinduon ka desh hai, aur Hindu larh hi nahin sakte. Unka Khyal hai ki Hindu kewal dharam karam, pooja, path ityadi mein lage rahte hain. Aur khas taur se voh dhoti-walon ko bilkul larhne ke kabil nahin samajhte. Baharhal, aap mein se to koi dhoti pahanta nahin, kintu main to dhoti pahantu hi hun*". And then quietly he remarked "*Par, mujhe yeh nahin malum ki jyada zordar faisle main ne dhoti pahan ke liye, ya President Ayub ne pant pahan kar*" (The Pakistanis feel that Hindus cannot fight. Although we keep stressing that Hindustan is the homeland of other communities also, they keep equating Hindustan with Hindus, whom they regard as incapable of fighting. Their belief is that Hindus are too pre-occupied with *Dharma* and *Karma* and *pooja* and *path* (religious recitation) etc. In particular, they have scorn for *dhotiwalas,* whom they put down as altogether useless as fighters. Of course, none of you wear *dhoties,* but I do. I wonder, however, whether more forceful decisions were taken by myself wearing a *dhoti* or by President Ayub clad in pants).

Another example of his humour was demonstrated at yet another such site within Pakistan where he was addressing the soldiers in the field. At these places, in order that the PM should be easily visible, a table was brought and put out (generally, a table with folding legs) and the PM stood upon it. Immediately the Corps Commander and the Divisional Commander stood on either side of him, and the poor table began to shake. When it was suggested to the Generals that they sit down and allow the PM to stand alone, they brushed it aside saying that military etiquette does not permit them to sit down when the PM is standing. So all three of them stood on the table which groaned and shook beneath their weight, and we could not help feeling uneasily that like in the case of Humpty Dumpty there was going to be a great fall. Shastriji himself must have shared this feeling, because once or twice he requested the Generals to sit down, whereupon they stood more firmly erect than before. So when addressing the soldiers, Shastriji remarked: "*Main chahta tha ki apne bahadur jawanon se milta, aur aap bhi apne Pradhan Mantri ko dekh lete. Aur meri bari khwahish thi ki is mauke par main aapke saamne kuch janchta. Lekin main kaise janch sakta hun, jab dahinen baen do khambhon ke saman aapke janaral sahiban kharhe hue hain*". (I wanted very much to meet our brave soldiers and also that you get an opportunity to see your Prime Minister. And it was my cherished wish that on this occasion I could look a little impressive. But how can I look impressive, when to the right and left of me your Generals are towering over me like two pillars?) He had only to say this when in the burst of laughter that followed, the two generals sheepishly jumped down and took their seats, military etiquette notwithstanding.

Another fine instance of his quiet humour was at Jaipur, when he was returning from a visit to Jodhpur, which had been heavily bombed during the war, and several people had been killed. There was a massive crowd at the Jaipur public meeting, which must have been over a million. There the Chief Minister, Rajasthan, Shri Mohan Lal Sukhadia announced amidst tremendous applause that he would weigh Shastriji in gold and donate the gold to the National Defence Fund for purchase of Gnat aircraft (the Gnat Aircraft had become the talk of the country after their successful shooting down of the U.S. gifted Pakistan Sabre Jets). Shastriji was flanked on either side by the Governor of Rajasthan, Dr. Sampurnanand, and the Chief Minister, Shri Sukhadia, both men of considerable girth and weight. When it came to his turn to speak, he warmly thanked the Chief Minister for the magnanimous offer, but went on to say: "*Yeh tulne tulane ki baat se mujhe kuch sankoch hota hai. Aur mujh jaise halke, phulke aadmi ko tol kar Raksha Kosh ko milega hi kya? Mere jo dahinen baen do Maharathi baithe hain, inme se kinhi ko aap toliye, to vastav mein desh ka bhala hoga*". (I feel a little hesitant about this business of being weighed. And by weighing so small and light a person like myself, what is the (National) Defence Fund going to get? Now if you were to weigh one of these two stalwarts who are sitting to the right and left of me, then indeed the country will be benefited.)

The end of the war with Pakistan was Shastriji's moment of supreme triumph. He became the hero of his people, and wherever he went lakhs and lakhs of people, turned out to see and hear him. Being only human, he could not help revelling in the glory. Once, some years earlier, at an All India Congress

Committee Session in Madurai in the South, when Pandit Nehru had arrived from the airport with cheering crowds all the way, and the streets lined with people and children throwing flowers, and he himself throwing flower garlands back at them in return, Shastriji had wistfully remarked "*Neta ho to aisa ho. Hum jaise tatpoonjiye hone se kya fayda*"? (If one should be a leader, he should be such a leader. What is the good of being trifling persons like ourselves?) That position and that acclaim he attained after the Pakistan War in the last few months of his life, and he could not but have gloried in it.

But at the same time he was too honest a person not to be struck by the incongruity of the situation. Here was he, a life long devotee of peace, a fervent believer in Gandhiji and *ahimsa*, who was being hailed as a great warrior and conqueror. There were even sycophantic poems, some of which compared him to Sikandar (Alexander the Great), and others to Alexander's opponent Puru (Porus). Deep inside, he had a feeling of some uneasiness about the strangeness of the situation. He reminded me very much of the first Superintendent of Police I had worked with, when I first held charge of a District as a District Magistrate in UP. The SP was a devout Jain, a strict vegetarian and a staunch follower of the tenets of his religion, which enshrined non-violence towards all living beings as the supreme embodiment of love and devotion. But when a dacoit gang was ravaging the district, the SP put himself at the head of his force, and in the encounter which followed, he personally shot dead the dacoit leader. And ever after, with a strange mixture of pride and remorse, he used to go around saying: "I am a Jain, and I have killed a man". That is somewhat how Shastriji was feeling on being acclaimed as a great war leader. And thus it was that when the first chance for an honourable peace came, he took it with both hands. His words to the Defence Minister, Shri Chavan, on leaving for Tashkent at Mr. Kosygin's invitation were: "We must now fight for Peace with the same determination with which we fought the War". He had led his nation to victory in war and had become the hero of his people, but in the end his life-long love of Peace prevailed, and the Man of Action became once again the Seeker after Peace, who sealed the Tashkent Declaration with his life.

CHAPTER 11

THE FRAIL MORTAL COIL AND THE DEMANDS OF THE SPIRIT

BUT EVEN as Shastriji drove himself onward and upward to ever greater heights, his health was not able to keep pace. He had suffered his first heart attack in October 1959, in Allahabad, when he was Minister of Commerce and Industry, and had to spend quite some time in the Hospital in the Civil Lines. He was nursed devotedly by Smt. Lalita Shastri, and I still remember the rich and touching tribute he paid to her. I was showing him a book with some pictures from Indian mythology with captions in English, and Smt. Shastri who had just come in, glanced at one of them and asked what it depicted: I replied that it was the picture of Savitri rescuing the soul of her dead husband, Satyavan, from Yama, the God of Death and bringing him back to life. Shastriji looked at his wife and gently remarked: "She has done the same thing for me", and I still remember the blush of joy and modesty which suffused the whole of Smt. Lalitaji's face.

His second instance of heart trouble came in June 1964 just after he had taken over as Prime Minister. This was a relatively mild one, but it was enough to keep him from attending the Conference of Commonwealth Prime Ministers in London. It was felt in political circles close to him that so soon after the vexed question of succession to Pandit Nehru had been so successfully resolved, it should not be disclosed that his chosen successor had just suffered a heart attack. So it was given out that the Prime Minister had been overcome by the heat and the strain and was suffering from exhaustion and fatigue and had been advised complete rest. In the effort to keep up this story even the Health Minister, Dr. Sushila Nayar, and the top doctors of the Health Organization were not permitted to visit and examine him and on her insistence they were somewhat brusquely told by Shri T.T. Krishnamachari not to interfere.

Shastriji's treatment was looked after by Colonel (later Major General) Moitra, the President's Physician, and his own doctor, Dr. R.N. Chugh, with the advice of the heart specialist, Dr. Dhanda. The net result was that the Health Minister and the senior doctors of the Health Organization were made to feel that they had nothing to do with the health of the Prime Minister, and were in no way responsible. They were not required to exercise any supervision or give any guidance to Dr. Chugh, who, though a very competent doctor, was rather young and relatively junior. This was to have grave and tragic consequences in the light of what later transpired at Tashkent.

So Shastriji treated these warning signals as of little consequence, and continued to work at full pressure without adequate rest or respite. He just did not know how to take things easy and play it cool, no matter how calm a demeanour he managed to present outwardly. About Pt. Nehru he used to remark admiringly that when Panditji attended some musical function he became totally absorbed in the music and kept beating time with his hands and feet and swaying his head (*Jhoomte rahte hain*). Shastriji, with a touch of envy used to say, "I do not know how he does it, considering the weight of problems he is carrying. I just cannot lose myself like that."

Shastriji experienced the full burden of Prime Ministership with little of its pleasures. In order to measure up to his great responsibilities he would not give himself the needed respite and relaxation, disregarding the advice of his doctors, who urged him to find some time in the day for lying down and resting. To such pleas his response used to be. "*Adhey lete, adhey baithe mujh-se kam nahin hoga, karoonga to theek se karoonga, varna chorh kar chala jaoonga*" (If I have to be PM, I must do my very best. I cannot function half sitting and half lying down. Either I will do it properly or else I will leave and go away). He believed fervently in Gandhiji's saying "When in office sit light not tight." The only exercise he was able to get was in walking up and down the lawn with his morning visitors. It was a common sight in the mornings to see the PM picking up one or two or three visitors and doing some rounds of the garden with them discussing matters, and then coming and picking the next lot for the combined stroll and discussion.

His only real relaxation was playing with his grand children, when for a brief while he would forget everything and give himself to them. But as the months passed and the burdens increased, even this had become less and less.

Part of the strain was brought on by his own goodness (maybe lack of firmness). For instance, when told that so and so (generally some important person) wanted to meet him, he would react with dismay, and say that if he comes he will take a good two hours; please try and save me. So ring after ring would come on the telephone, and we would keep saying 'Sorry, sir, the PM is busy, he is just not available" and so on. Ultimately, reaching the point of exasperation, the person would one day virtually force his way into the PM's room, and the moment he entered the PM would stand up to receive him with words like "*Aieye, aieye, bahut dinon se aapke darshan nahin hue.*" (Come in, come in, it is long since we have met.) The result was that people went around saying that the PM is such a jewel of a person, but he is surrounded by a set of wicked people on his staff.

But a major part of the strain was brought on by the pressure of public engagements from which we as a people do not believe in sparing our leaders. Apart from the inexorable round of inaugurations and foundation-stone layings etc. there are so many trivial insistences that sap their time and energy. Somebody writes a book, the PM must write the foreword; some film is having its first showing, the PM must perform the *muhurat;* some one is getting married, the PM must come to bless the happy pair. The Chief Ministers, when they met Shastriji, would be so solicitous, "Shastriji, you must take good care of your health, your life is so precious for the nation." and so forth. Yet when they succeeded in inviting him to their State, they drew up programmes which would have invalided even the healthiest of men—hedge-hopping from airfield to airfield, addressing vast crowds at every stop, streams of visitors and meetings, functions going on till late into the night, etc. This seems to be a national trait, this hypocrisy, telling our top leaders how precious their lives are, and then loading them down with needless pressures and engagements which would tend to shorten those very lives.

So Lal Bahadurji drove himself on smiling and waving, but there was such a difference between the outward appearance and the inward reality. How long could the frail mortal coil put up with the demands of the spirit? Those of us who were near him were filled with occasional forebodings. He seemed to be living in terms of the poem:

I burnt my candle at both ends
It will not last the night
But oh my friends, and ah my foes
It gives a lovely light."

Despite his frail constitution and indifferent health, he managed to carry on for sometime, because power is its own oxygen. But sometimes even this would not suffice. On his return from Burma on the 24th of December 1965 he had stopped to preside over the Vishwabharati Convocation in Shantiniketan. When I took his draft address to him late at night for his perusal and approval, I was myself shocked at his appearance. He looked utterly worn out and haggard. The emptiness and weariness of ages seemed to be on his face. I had expressed my forebodings to some of my colleagues on the Personal Staff, that people hardly realized the terrible strain through which he was passing, and that one day he might pass away like a candle going out, and the world would wake up to find that he had gone. And that is precisely what happened at Tashkent on that terrible night of 10/11th January, 1966, when triumph was followed by tragedy and a shocked and unbelieving world woke up in a grey dawn of weeping.

CHAPTER 12

TASHKENT: TRIUMPH OVERSHADOWED BY TRAGEDY

DURING HIS occasional musings the Prime Minister once or twice referred to an incident that and taken place as far back as 1927 or so, when he was a young worker of the Servants of People Society. He was travelling by train from Meerut to Muzaffarnagar in Western UP, and on the opposite bench there was a gentleman who appeared to be a South Indian, and who kept staring at the young Lal Bahadur, almost to the point of rudeness. After sometime the gentleman spoke and said. "You must be thinking it very rude of me to stare at you like this, but in your forehead, I see the signs of greatness. You will rise very high and become a very famous man." The young Lal Bahadur modestly said that having joined politics he might come to be known at the District and possibly later even at the Provincial level. The gentleman replied. "No, no, it is some thing far higher than that. At this Shastriji smiled sceptically and said. "If you are meaning the National level permit me to be a little sceptical, because I am only a humble worker and know my limitations". At which the gentleman replied: "Not only the National level, but the International level." And he added: "I know you do not believe a word of what I say and think I am off my mind. But I shall tell you one more thing whether you believe it or not. One day you will die in a foreign land, far from your family and loved ones." The Prime Minister used to say that: "I wonder whether that gentleman is still alive, and whether in the Prime Minister of today, he recalls the humble youth of 1927". And sometimes he would reflect: "I wonder whether the second part of the prophecy is also going to come true." and then of course, we would rush in to say that sometimes these matters are pure coincidence, and that in any case the second part could hardly come true, because Mataji (Smt. Shastri) never let him go abroad alone. And yet, the second part of the prophecy was also to come dreadfully true, and it did come to pass that he died in a foreign land far from his family and loved ones.

How it happened that no member of his family was by his side on that fatal visit to Tashkent is a sad story in itself. At first Smt. Shastri was to accompany him, but he dissuaded her by saying that the winter cold would be very severe, and since he would be busy in the crucial negotiations from morning till night, she would be left all alone to herself. When even then she insisted, he said that he was going for such agonizingly crucial negotiations on which the fate of the country depended, and people would say he had brought his wife along '*tafrih ke liye*' (for enjoyment and pleasure). The use of the word *tafrih* wounded her, and she asked whether she had been having *tafrih* with him during their life together with so many hardships and sacrifices. Shastriji immediately realized his thoughtless use of the word and expressed regret. However, Smt. Shastri in a decision which she has never ceased to regret, decided to stay back in accordance with his wishes. But she asked her second son Anil (pet name 'Pappu' and until recently an M.P. and Deputy Minister, Finance, in the Government of India) to go with his father. However, on the night before leaving for Tashkent, Shastriji came back from office and said that he had decided to go alone. The boy had made all preparations to go and was deeply hurt. Early next morning when Shastriji was leaving for the airport, he noticed that Anil was not there (The whole family used to go to the airport and touch his feet before he emplaned) He immediately went in and found the boy lying in bed. Shastriji realized how hurt he must be feeling, and placing his finger under the boy's chin in an affectionate gesture, he asked him to forgive him for this time, but promised that "when I go to the USA towards the end of January, I will definitely take you along".

Since it had come about that no member of his family was accompanying him to Tashkent, his attendant of many years, Shri Ram Nath, was strictly enjoined to take every care of the Prime Minister. The doctors had said clearly that he should not be left all to himself, especially at night. The family knew that Ram Nath could not sleep in the Prime Minister's room—it was hardly possible to put another bed beside the PM's, and being what he was, Shastriji just would not think of allowing Ram Nath to sleep on the floor even on thick carpets. Earlier efforts to put Ram Nath in the bedroom had failed, because Shastriji, to avoid the man's sleeping on the floor in his room, said that "he snores a lot and disturbs me". So, since Ram Nath could not be in the PM's bedroom, he was asked to sleep in the adjacent room so as to be readily available. But it was mid-winter in Tashkent and bitterly cold, and the Russians had provided a heated bed room for Ram Nath in the upper storey. When about 12.30 a.m. on 11th January, the PM asked Ram Nath to desist from further packing for the morning flight to Kabul and go to sleep, he went upstairs to his warm and cosy cubicle. Thus it was that at the fatal moment, when Shastriji got his heart attack, there was no one near at hand whom he could call for help.

Before coming to the events of that fatal night of 10th/11th January 1966 one might touch briefly on the sequence of events in Tashkent leading up to it. These have been graphically described by one who was present, Shri Jagannath Sahai, Assistant Private Secretary to the PM, who had put in long and devoted years of service with Shastriji (later he was attached to the President of India, Dr Zakir Husain, and after him to Shri Khurshid Alam Khan, when he was in the Central Council of Ministers).

Shastriji had declared before leaving India for Tashkent that not an inch of Indian territory would be surrendered to Pakistan. But in Tashkent he found himself under tremendous pressure for complete vacation of all territories captured during the fighting, including those in Pakistan-occupied Kashmir, which India regarded as its own territory. Mr Kosygin, the Prime Minister of the USSR, who was acting as the mediator made it clear that nothing short of this would suffice for a settlement. When the talks appeared to be heading for a deadlock, Mr. Kosygin called on the Prime Minister on the night of the 9th January around 10.30 p.m. and spent quite some time with him. Immediately thereafter, Shastriji called for an early morning meeting at 8.00 a.m. the following day (10th January) of all the Ministers and Senior Officers forming the Indian delegation.

Shortly before the meeting, when Shri Jagannath Sahai looked into the PM's room, he found him with a piece of paper on which he had written in his own hand the well-known Urdu couplet:

> *Barhe shauk se sun raha tha Zamana*
> *Hum hi so gaye dāstan kahate kahate*
>
> (The world was listening with the greatest of interest. Only I myself went off to sleep even while narrating the tale).

In the light of what happened later that very night, these words proved to be poignantly prophetic.

Evidently it was at this morning meeting of 10th January that it was decided to accept Mr. Kosygin's suggestions for a settlement. For thereafter, that very afternoon President Ayub Khan came for lunch with the Prime Minister and spent over two hours with him. There were no Aides present, and it was a very cordial meeting.

President Ayub invited the Prime Minister to overfly Pakistan on the way back home (on the outward journey he had to avoid Pakistan by a long detour over the Arabian Sea and Iran). To this Shastriji thankfully agreed.

The signing of the historic Declaration took place at 4.00 p.m. Everyone was in high spirits, save only the Pakistan Foreign Minister, Mr. Zulfikar Ali Bhutto, who looked glum and never once smiled. Shastriji himself was in a very good mood, but later when he spoke to the Indian journalists present in an impromptu Press Conference in the same building, he was in a more subdued mood.

After the grand reception hosted by Mr. Kosygin to celebrate the signing of the Declaration, Shastriji returned to his dacha (villa). He said he had eaten all sorts of things at the Reception, his stomach felt heavy, and he did not want to eat anything. However, he was persuaded to take some *Alu-Palak* (potatoes and spinach) which Ram Nath had prepared, with two pieces of toast. Later at night, when the glass of milk was brought he again expressed a disinclination to take it, but was persuaded to take half a glass.

Shri Sahai had contacted the PM's residence on the telephone on the hot line which had been installed between Tashkent and

Delhi. Shastriji asked about the general reaction in the country to the Agreement. When told of the criticism voiced by some Opposition M.P.s, he said that it was only natural for those in the Opposition to be critical. He wanted to speak to his wife, but she could not make out anything in view of the disturbed condition of the line. So he spoke to his elder daughter, Kusum. She referred to the reaction of dismay at the handing back of the strategic Haji Pir Pass in Kashmir and the strong feeling that the Pass, captured at the cost of so much Indian blood and lives, should not have been given back in this manner. She also said that the whole family, including her mother, shared these sentiments. Shastriji appeared somewhat dismayed, but remarked that there were certain compulsions in the situation and he would explain the whole position on his return. He also asked for the next morning's newspapers to be flown to Kabul where he was proceeding from Tashkent, so that he could have a first-hand account of the country's reaction to the Tashkent Agreement—little dreaming that the next morning's newspapers would be carrying banner headlines of his death.

After the telephone call he kept strolling in his room, and that was when the last living photograph of him was taken—a profile through the window from outside the building.

Despite the lateness of the night, in view of the departure for Kabul early the next morning, Shri Sahai and the P.A., Shri M.M.N. Sharma, were awake and completing their packing. All of a sudden at 1.20 a.m. the Prime Minister appeared at the door of their room with his hands on his chest, and asked "Doctor Sahib Kahan hain? (Where's the doctor?) Seeing his obvious discomfort, they called out to Dr Chugh to come at once, and the DSP Security, Shri R. Kapur, and the PA took hold of the PM and escorted him back to his bedroom, while the Assistant PS rushed to the telephone to seek help.

On the way back the PM started coughing, and it was a dry coughing with a choking sound. Once back in the bedroom they tried to get him to lie down, but the distress had become so acute that he could not even remain lying but sat up, and when he could not even remain sitting, he stood up restlessly with his hands on his chest, while agonized exclamations of "*Hai Ram, hai baap*" kept escaping his lips. All those who knew his iron control over his feelings and emotions could easily understand the extent of pain and agony he must have been suffering. With great difficulty the staff got him to lie down, and he appeared to be calming down, but actually he was sinking. At this stage the doctor burst into the room, and immediately tried desperately to do everything possible to revive him by giving injections, doing massage, and even mouth to mouth respiration. But it was too late. The events moved so quickly in those dreadful few minutes. At 1.20 a.m. the Prime Minister had appeared at the doctor's door with his hands on his chest. At. 1.32 a.m. he lay dead in his bed.

So the doctor and the Personal Staff found themselves at dead of night with a dead Prime Minister, and no one near-by from whom they could seek help, because the only persons present, the Russian security guards, spoke no English, leave alone Hindi. It was only when they kept calling out desperately on the telephone that those outside realized that something seriously amiss had occurred. But by the time everyone arrived, including the top heart specialists whom the Russian Government had kept ready at Tashkent, it was far too late to do anything. All the efforts of the doctors to revive Shastriji, including hand massage of the heart, were in vain. There was nothing to do—save to break the shocking news to a grief-stricken world, which only a few hours previously had hailed with relief and joy the historic Tashkent Declaration.

What happened in Tashkent on that fateful night is tragic in the extreme. Even more unfortunate is the fact that there are some controversies regarding the circumstances of his death. There was some discussion in Parliament as to why Shastriji had to go himself to seek help, and why if, as stated, there was a telephone by his bedside, he did not use the same. A reply was given that we are talking of the Prime Minister of India, and if he did not choose to use the telephone what was there that anybody else could have done about it. Such remarks did injustice to Shastriji. There was a telephone with a long cord in the suite of the Prime Minister, on the lifting of the receiver of which, a buzzer would sound in the room occupied by the Personal Staff. The telephone could be placed in the bedroom or in the long sitting room where the main sofas were right across the room, well away from the bedroom door. That night the telephone was not in the bedroom. It was in the sitting room at some distance from the bedroom door. Anyone in distress at dead of night would, rather than walk up to the Telephone to sound the buzzer, which might or might not be heard by sleeping persons, seek the safer course of walking to the door of the room where the Staff were residing, which is what Shastriji apparently did.

A heart patient when suffering from an attack is not expected to move even his little finger, if it can be avoided. In the case of the Prime Minister of India, he had to get up and walk all that distance to seek help, and be walked back again. Whatever chance of life there may have been, must have been lost in the process.

There are some who believe that there had been foul play and he had been poisoned—a belief shared by Smt. Shastri and his family. In his dying moments he had pointed to the flask of water by his bedside. Those with him thought he wanted to drink, but he could not or would not. His pointing to the flask of water, and his refusal (or inability) to drink the water therefrom is believed to have been his dying effort to point to the source of mischief. When Smt. Shastri and the family visited Tashkent some months later, and I accompanied them, it could be seen that the Russians had till that time kept everything in the room as it was at the time of his death, even to the used towel and soap in the bathroom. But the flask of water at the bedside was not there.

Be that as it may, there are others who felt that Shastriji's telephonic conversation with the family and his learning of the unfavourable reaction to some aspects of the Agreement, especially the vacation of the Haji Pir Pass and other recaptured areas of Pakistan-occupied Kashmir despite his firm declaration to the contrary, so weighed upon the Prime Minister's mind that it must have contributed to bringing on the heart attack. Despite the anxiety he must have been feeling, this appears unlikely. Shastriji was one who, when convinced, never shirked taking difficult and even unpopular decisions—the Kutch crisis is an example. Apprehension about unfavourable public reaction to a course of action he felt unavoidable and correct in the circumstances could hardly have upset him to this extent.

More to the point, it is said that the PM had not been physically examined on that last day. No doubt, he had been extremely busy from early morning. But in view of the tension and strain of that day, some opportunity could and should have been taken for a check-up. According to some doctors, digestive upset can be a fore-runner of impending heart trouble. He had complained of heaviness in the stomach following his return from Mr. Kosygin's Reception, but in the euphoria of the moment, this, which might perhaps have given some warning of what was to come, was not acted upon.

All said and done, it is unfortunate that the sudden death of a Prime Minister in such circumstances was not made the subject of high-level inquiry. The Russian doctors and Dr. Chugh of course issued a signed medical bulletin detailing their unsuccessful efforts to revive him, and attributing the death to heart failure, "acute myocardial infarction" The statements of those who were with him at the Dacha (Villa) were recorded but never disclosed. Partly the reason may have been so as not to embarrass the host foreign government. But the Russian Government too could perhaps have been associated with any inquiry. In any case, there do not appear to have been lapses on their part. The excellent medical arrangements made by them in the In-tourist Hostel building where the PM was originally to stay had been nullified by the sudden change of his residence to the lonely Villa by members of his own party less then twenty four hours before the PM's arrival in Tashkent. And this was done despite the advice of the head of his Security, Shri G.C. Dutt, Joint Director, Intelligence Bureau, who had reached a few days earlier and decided on the arrangements for stay after taking all the circumstances into account. Moreover, knowing Shastriji to be a heart patient, the Russians had kept ready in Tashkent some of their very good heart specialisits. It is another matter that no one had chosen to maintain liaison with them, as happens in the case of security arrangements, where the security officers accompanying a VIP immediately seek out and maintain close liaison throughout with their counterparts in the host country. However, despite all this, the comment of the common people of Tashkent is of interest. Shortly after Shastriji's death and before Smt. Shastri's visit, Tashkent had been rocked by a number of earthquake tremors, and many parts of the city had suffered heavy damage. One of the few areas completely spared was the area around the dacha where the Prime Minister had stayed. While Smt. Shastri was at Tashkent a comment could be heard among the common people, some of whom, despite communism, had not completely shed their faith in religion (Islam), that this was God's punishment for what had been done to that great and good man.

It is a sad fact that in the minds of quite a number of persons, there is still some doubt about the circumstances leading to his death. But even if one rules out deliberate mischief, one cannot dispel the impression that there appears to have been negligence on a scale which was astounding, and some of it should have been culpable. There are so many unanswered questions:

> Why was the PM's place to stay suddenly changed just 24 hours before his arrival in Tashkent in spite of the advice of his Security in-charge?
>
> Why was he put up in a lonely villa some 2-3 furlongs away from where the rest of the party were staying and where the Russians had provided excellent medical arrangements?
>
> Why apart from his personal doctor, were there no medical arrangements at the villa?
>
> Why was full liaison not maintained with the heart specialists and other top medical men whom the Russians had kept ready in Tashkent?
>
> Whether full quota of portable life-saving instruments were in fact available with the PM's doctor?
>
> Why had the Prime Minister not been physically checked up on the day of the occurrence?
>
> Why following his return from Mr. Kosygin's Reception, certain signs which might have given some warning were not acted upon?
>
> Why was it not ensured that the telephone was placed in his bedroom that night?

All these questions needed to be looked into in depth, but perhaps it was felt better that with the Prime Minister himself dead and gone, these inconvenient questions could also rest with him. Anyway, I who was not myself present in Tashkent on that fateful visit, have no desire to fan the embers of controversy regarding the death of one, who all his life had done his best to steer clear of controversy.

In all this controversy, what is undoubted and touching is the tribute paid to him by his former adversary, the President of

Pakistan, whom he had fought so bitterly a few months earlier. As disclosed by Shri Jagannath Sahai, at 4.00 a.m. on that sad morning, President Ayub Khan paid an unscheduled and unexpected visit. He stood for a few minutes in silence by the bedside, gazing at the body of Shastriji, his erstwhile enemy. He then remarked: "This man has laid down his life for the sake of peace between the two countries. I know he wanted Peace."

CHAPTER 13

"THIS WAS A MAN"

So Shastriji passed away into history. He died at the height of his fame and glory, leaving his countrymen weeping over his loss. For him it was a death with honour; for his country his passing was a tragedy and a calamity. Just when he had really come into his own after months of struggle, just when like a newly-risen sun he was dominating the Indian firmament, just when his countrymen were looking up to him with gratitude and with eager hope and expectation, just at that time he vanished from the scene like a lamp going out, leaving behind darkness and desolation. The history of this country would have been very different if he had been spared just a few years longer.

Posterity will continue to remember the greatness of this "great little man". Perhaps the Government of this country did not do all it could have to perpetuate his memory. For a time it seemed as if the Government of the U.S.S.R. was more concerned to do him honour. His statue was put up at one of the most important intersections in Tashkent where eight roads met, and which was named after him. A bronze plaque bearing his profile was put up on the outside wall of the villa where he had stayed, and for quite sometime his rooms were kept just as they had been at the time of his death. The affection and esteem with which the leaders and people of Tashkent greeted Smt. Lalita Shastri and the members of his family when they visited Tashkent some months after his death, had to be seen to be believed. In India, on the other hand, there seemed to be a down-playing of his role. On the 15th of August 1965 he had uttered from the ramparts of the Red Fort those challenging words which rang in a nation's ears; on the 15th of August 1966 his family were not even invited to the Red Fort function. There were even those who sought to propagate the impression that the nineteen months of his Prime Ministership were perhaps an unavoidable and unfortunate interregnum, much in the nature of Oliver Cromwell coming between the Stuarts in England, and that there was a fortunate Restoration of the Nehru era with the daughter taking the place of the father. For creating a Lal Bahadur Shastri National Memorial Trust, a Steering Committee was indeed set up with the President and Vice-President of India as its President and Vice-President, but despite a series of meetings the Trust never got off the ground. In a more modest manner Smt. Shastri had to set up the Shastri Seva Niketan at Manda in Allahabad District in what had been his constituency, with the help of the Raja of Manda, Shri Vishwanath Pratap Singh, the former Prime Minister.

Be that as it may, irrespective of anything that Governments may or may not have done, the common people of India and of the world continue to cherish the memory of one whom they regard as one of their own. In India people think of him as one who was just like themselves, and who would have saved the country from many of the embarrassments and hardships into which she was subsequently plunged. In other countries of the world, and there are many to which I have travelled, the mere mention of my association with Lal Bahadurji has evoked a flood of warmth and goodwill, as well as requests for more information about him.

His own life, I think, can best be described in two very apt and beautiful quotations from Shakespeare:

> ". . . Hath borne his faculties so meek
> Hath been so clear in his great office
> That his virtues will plead
> Like angels trumpet-tongued. . ."

Again, in the moving words of Mark Antony, pronounced over the dead body of Marcus Brutus on the battlefield of Phillipi:

> . . . His life was gentle
> And the elements so mixed in him
> That Nature might stand up and say to all the world
> 'This was a Man'

Though the name of Lal Bahadur Shastri will always be an honoured name in India's history, those of us who were his contemporaries, and more so those of us who were privileged to be associated with him, will remember more his warm, endearing human qualities, his goodness and kindness, his gentle courtesy and touching humility, his consideration and compassion for others. There is a sense of sweet sadness, as well as an aching void, when one thinks of him and of what might have been. His was a life that even after extinction leaves not only a halo but a fragrance behind, and our own lives will always be the richer and the fuller and the sweeter for having come into contact with his own.

I earnestly hope and fervently pray that something of that richness, that fullness, that sweetness will touch for a while the lives of those who happen to read these glimpses from the life of one who was among India's great men, but who was, even more essentially, one of God's good men.

Appendix

ORIGINAL LETTER in Hindi dated the 6th October 1963 by Shri Lal Bahadur Shastri to Shri Rajeshwar Prasad referred to in Chapter 2.

LAL BAHADUR SHASTRI

1, YORK PLACE
NEW DELHI

अक्तूबर 6, 1963

प्रिय राजेश्वर प्रसाद जी,

नमस्कार। आपका 2 सितम्बर का पत्र समय पर मिल गया था और 28 सितम्बर का कल मिला। खेद है कि पहले आपको न लिख सका। पिछले एक मास में अधिक व्यस्त रहना पड़ा है। इधर नये मुख्य मंत्रियों का चुनाव और उनकी कैबिनेट आदि के सम्बन्ध में भी बहुत समय लगा। उत्तर-प्रदेश के झगड़े को हम अभी तक नहीं सुलझा पाये। वहाँ की स्थिति से चिन्ता होती है। प्रदेश को कितनी क्षति पहुँच रही है वह प्रदेश के साथी कम ही अनुभव कर रहे हैं। परस्पर की व्यक्तिगत होड़ लगी हुई है।

पंडित जी ने बहुत चाहा कि मैं अपने पद पर बना रहूँ। कहा भी कई बार परन्तु पद से हटना मुझे अच्छा लगा। दूसरे को उपदेश देते देते और स्वयं कुछ न करने की कसक मेरे मन में रहती थी। जिस तेजी से कांग्रेस में हम नीचे की ओर खिसक रहे हैं वह भयावह मालूम देता है। गवर्नमेन्ट का शासन जिलों में वेग से निम्न स्तर की ओर जा रहा है। कोई स्वस्थ विरोधी दल बन नहीं पाया है। ऐसी स्थिति में यदि हम सरकार से बाहर आकर कुछ कर सकें तो पद त्याग का स्वागत ही करना चाहिए।

अभी तक तो लक्षण बहुत अच्छे नहीं दिखाई दिये हैं। परन्तु प्रारम्भ में यह बड़ा कदम कुछ दुविधा उत्पन्न करे तो आश्चर्य ही क्या। हम जो कुछ अनुभवी और बुज़ुर्ग माने जाते हैं उनका इम्तेहान है। मैं तो समझता हूँ कि दोष हमारा है, न कि हमारे प्रदेश अथवा ज़िले के कांग्रेस कार्यकर्ताओं का। अगले कुछ महीने यह स्पष्ट कर देंगे कि हमारी कितनी उपयोगिता बाहर है। मैं निराश नहीं हूँ।

कठिनाइयां तो घर में उठानी ही पड़ेंगी। आदमी अपने को साध ही लेता है।

मकान अभी बदला नहीं है पर छोटे मकान में जाऊँगा। एक सब्जी कम कर दी गयी है, दुध भी, कपड़ा भी थोड़ा हाथ से धोने लगे हैं, राम जी की मोटर इस्तेमाल करता हूँ। पैट्रोल अपना दूँगा। और भी बातें सम्भल कर करनी पड़ेंगी। दो बार पहले हट चुका हूँ, यह तीसरा नम्बर है। पिछले दो बार से इस बार तो सुविधायें कुछ अधिक ही हैं। हरि भी काम में लगे हुये हैं और संसद का भी अलाउन्स है। हाँ, खर्च का बोझ जरूर बढ़ गया है। सच तो यह है कि मेरी पत्नी का सच्चा और अनुपम सहयोग है और उनसे बड़ा बल तथा सहारा मिलता है अतएव चल ही जायेगा। आप लोगों का चिन्तित होना स्वाभाविक है। आगे की कम सोचना जान पड़ता है अच्छा है। यह विश्वास-सा होता है कि जो वह करता है वह हमें सहर्ष स्वीकार करना है :

हारियें न हिम्मत, बिसारिये न राम को।
जाहि विधि राखे राम ताहि विधि रहिये॥

2 अक्तूबर को हम लोग राजघाट गये थे। पुराना ही दृश्य था सिवाय समाधि पर नये निर्माण के। गांधी जी की याद रुला देती है। हम सब आराम और पदों की लालसा में पड़े हैं। पदों द्वारा सेवा और अर्चना की भावना कम है। गांधी जी का वैराग्य दृढ़ था। कबीर का पद उनके जीवन की झांकी है:

दास कबीरा जतन से ओढ़ी, ज्यों की त्यों धर दीनी चदरिया।

राजघाट पर पंडित जी को मेरे जन्म दिन की भी याद आ गयी। थोड़ी सी बात *नवभारत* में इस प्रकार प्रकाशित हुई:

"गांधी जी का जन्मदिन सब का जन्मदिन"

नई दिल्ली–2 अक्तूबर : सवेरे राजघाट पर श्री नेहरू ने शास्त्री जी से पूछा "सुना है आज तुम्हारा जन्मदिन है"। शास्त्री जी ने जो आम तौर से यह बात बताते नहीं हैं, कहा "आज तो गांधी जी का जन्मदिन है और उसी से मेरा ही क्यों सब का जन्मदिन है।"

आप तथा आपकी पत्नी स्वस्थ और खुश हैं यह जानकर प्रसन्नता हुयी। आप नये अनुभव और नयी जानकारी ले कर आएंगे। सरकार और देश के लिये अधिक उपयोगी होंगे। मैं जानता हूँ कि आप ने प्रत्येक क्षण का सुन्दर उपयोग किया होगा। अभी से आप हम सब की बधाई ले लें। अजय, आलोक, रवि व अन्शु सभी अच्छे हैं। दो बार यहाँ भी खाने पर आये थे। महेश्वर प्रसाद जी के यहाँ खाने पर सब मिले थे। बड़ी अच्छी तरह रह रहे हैं यद्यपि उनका मन आप दोनों के बिना अतृप्त ही रहता होगा और वे आप की बाट ही जोहते होंगे। आप और शायद आप से

अधिक आप की पत्नी उनको देखने के लिए अधीर होंगी। सोचती होंगी चलने का दिन जल्द ही क्यों नहीं आ जाता। आप के बड़े भाई साहब से भी भेंट हुई थी। महेश्वर प्रसाद जी अभी गृह मंत्रालय में ही हैं।

और सब कुशल हैं।

आपका

(लाल बहादुर)

श्री राजेश्वर प्रसाद जी
7, प्रिन्स एलबर्ट रोड
लन्दन, एन डब्ल्यू-1

INDEX